Cuter Than An

INTRAUTERINE:

The #BeaADay Coloring Book

First Edition

MIKE DENISON

Copyright © 2016 Mike Denison

ISBN: 0692685960
ISBN-13: 978-0692685969

For Andy Devlin
"Embrace Your Awesome"

1. #BeAADay

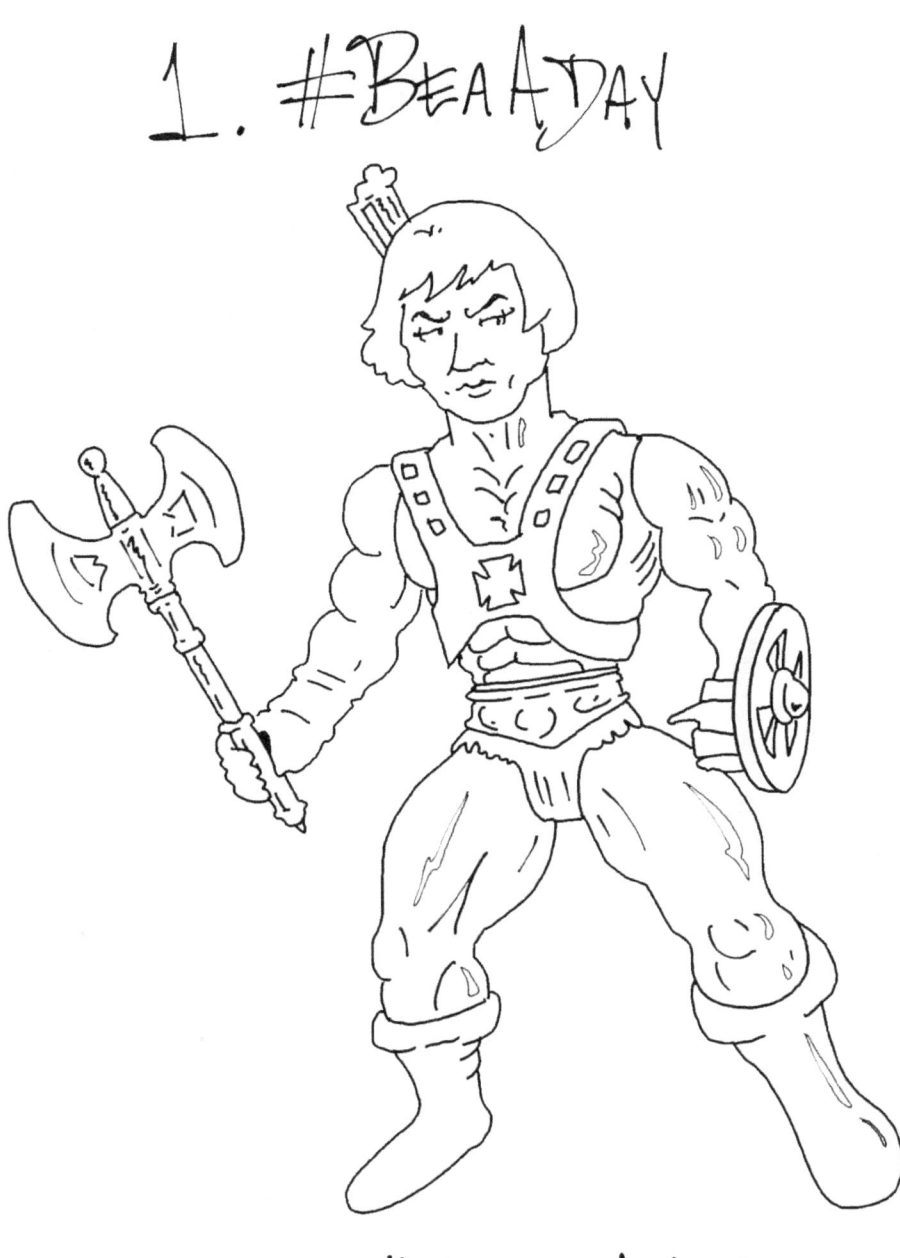

"BEA-MAN"

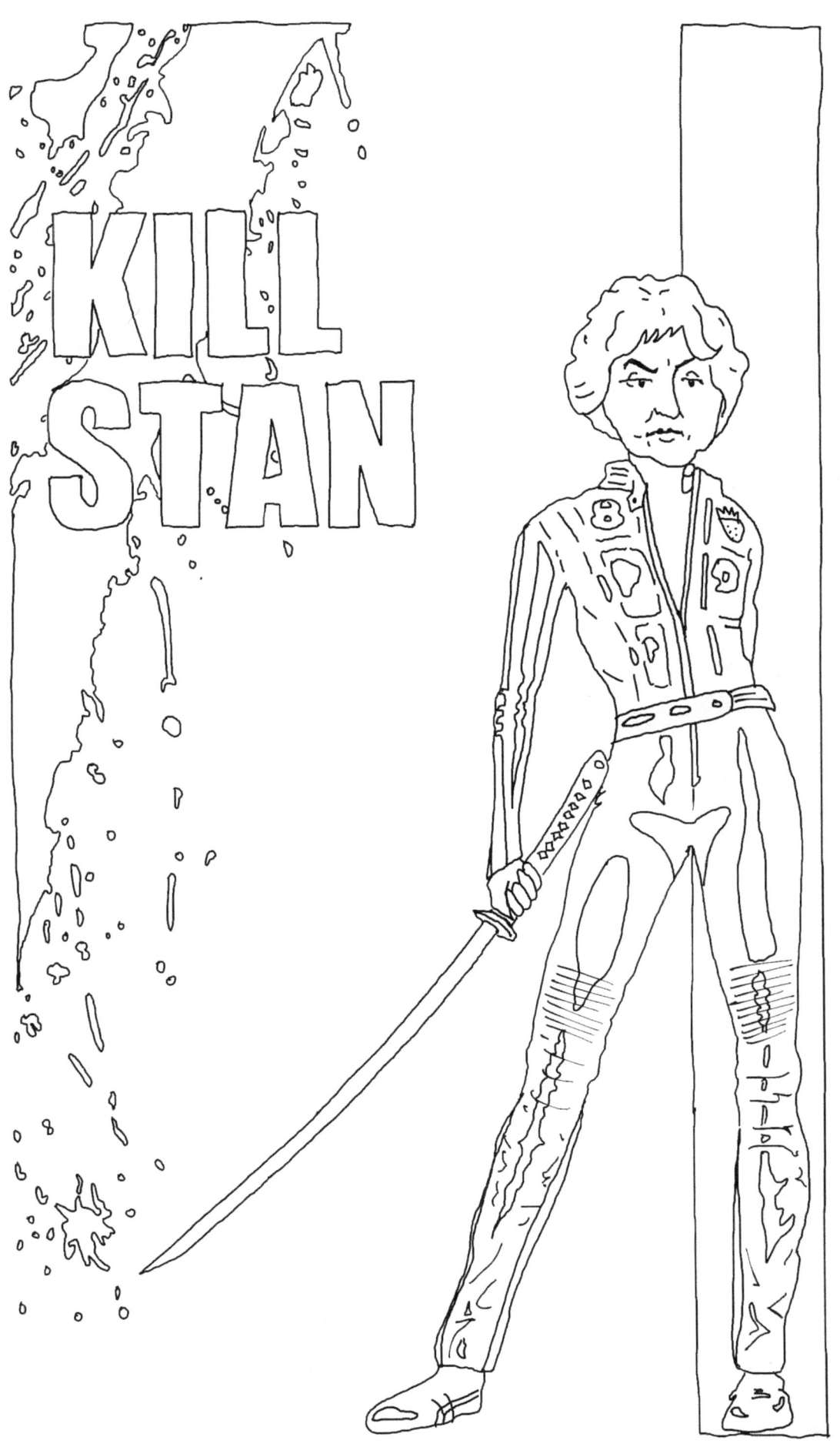

KILL STAN

THE POWERPUFF GOLDEN GIRLS

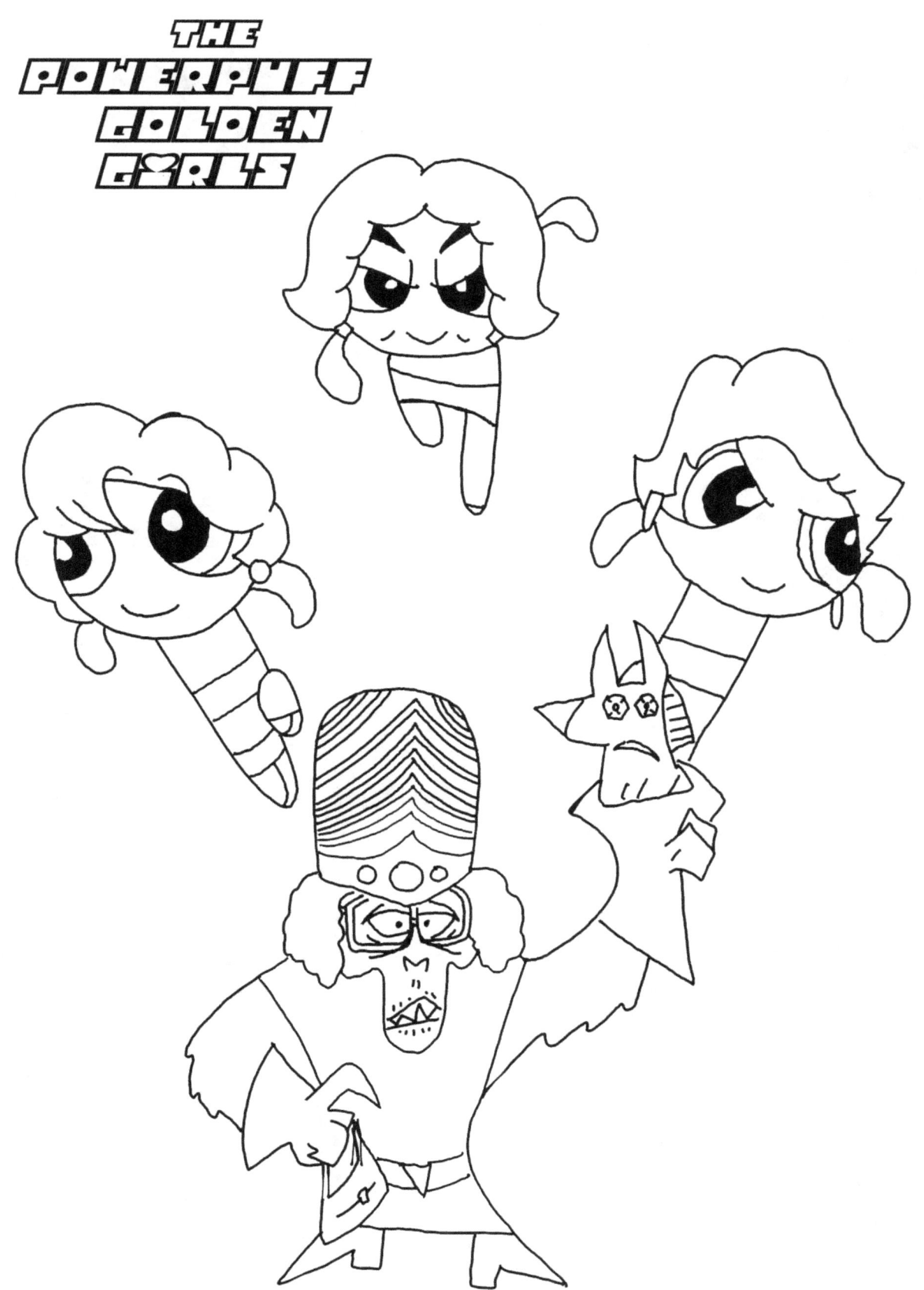

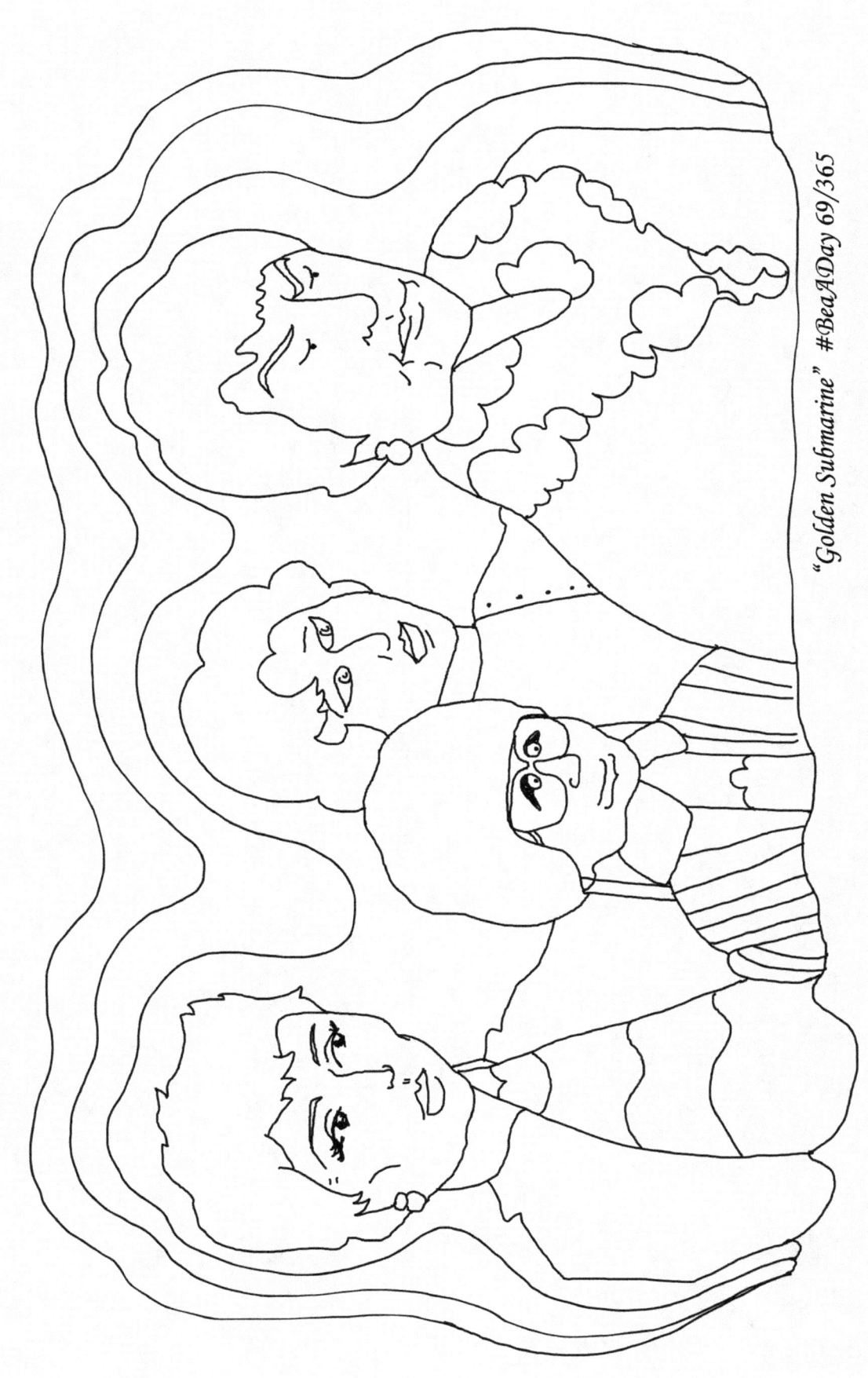

"Golden Submarine" #BeaADay 69/365

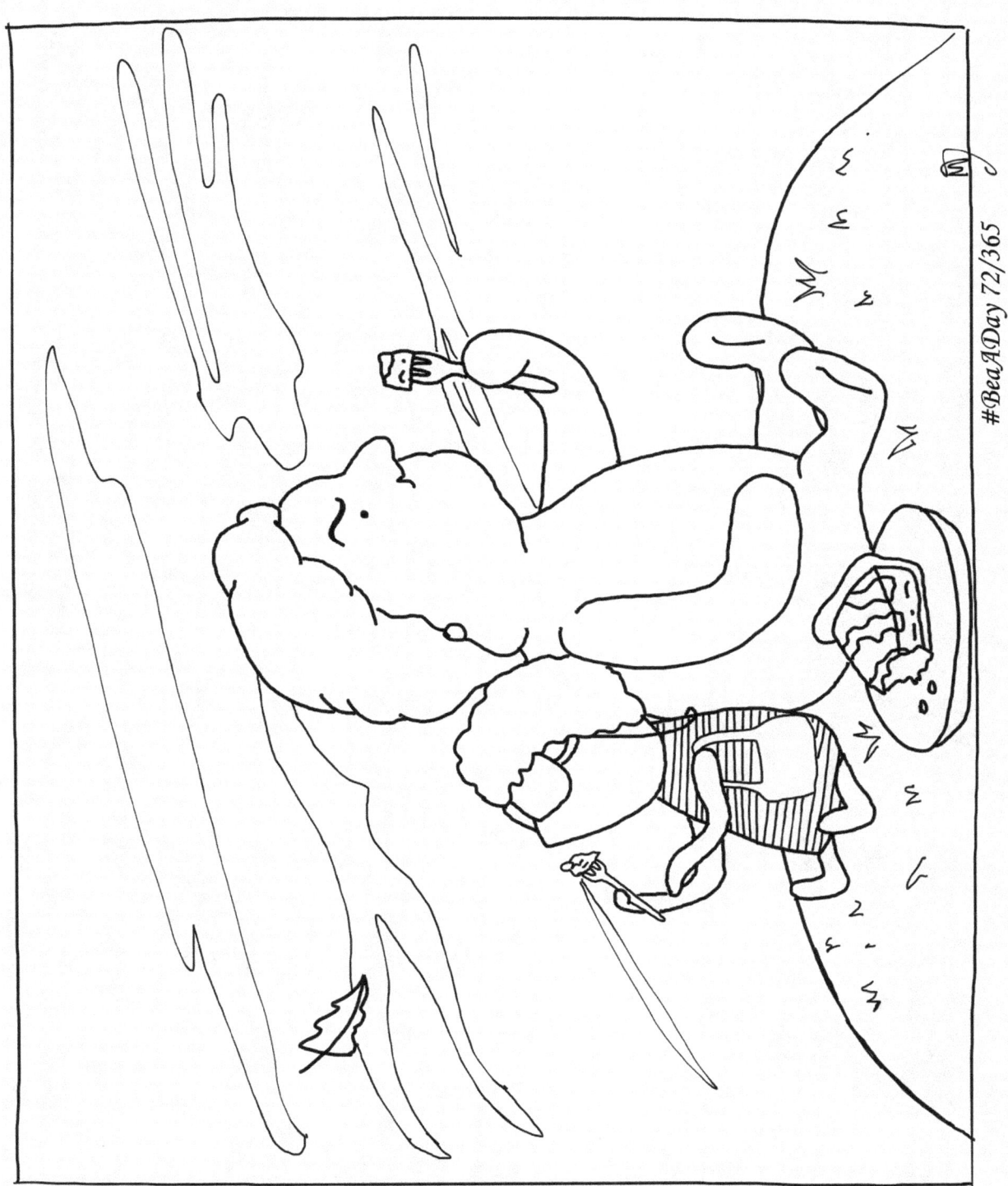

#BeaADay 72/365

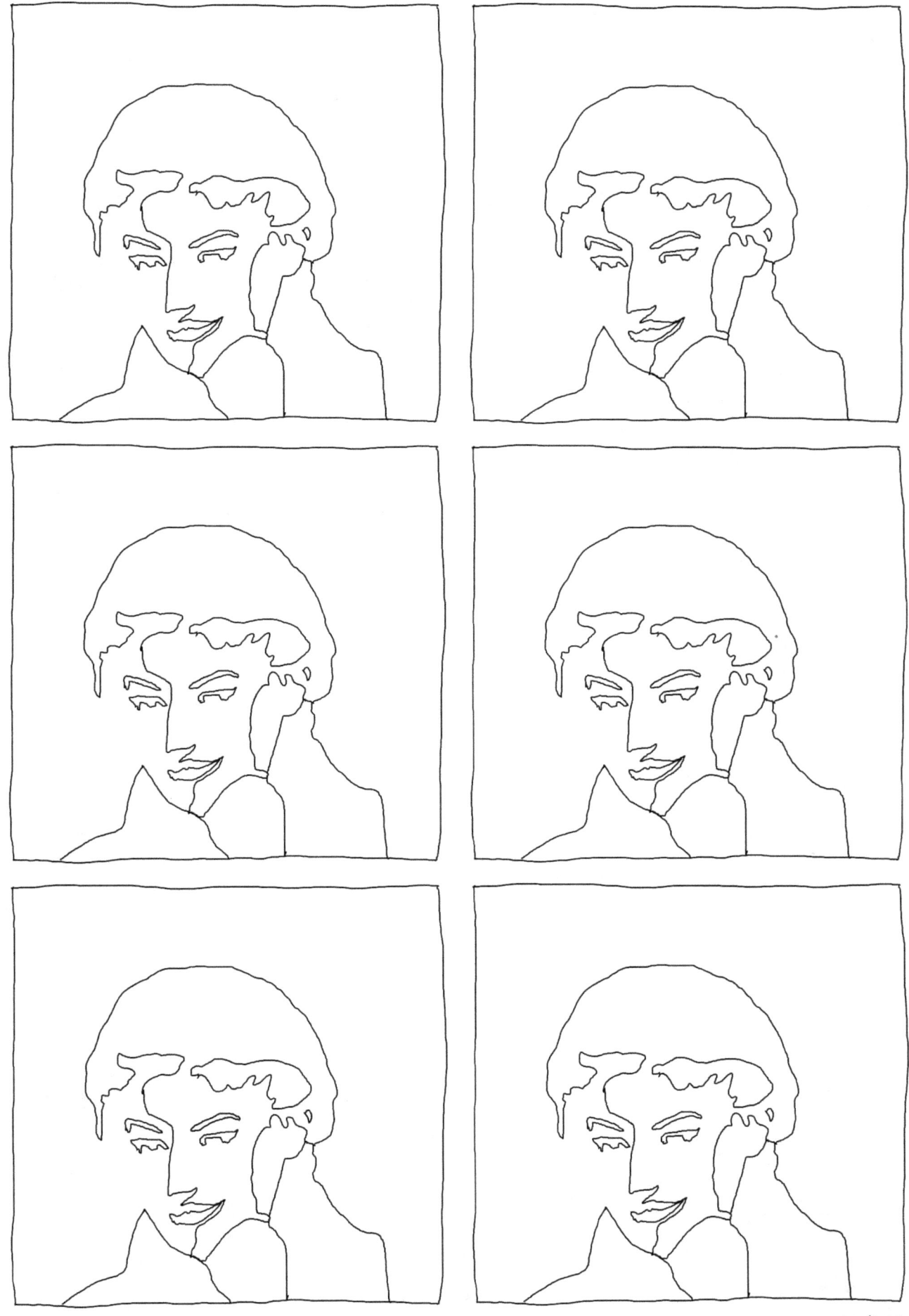

#BeaADay 87/365

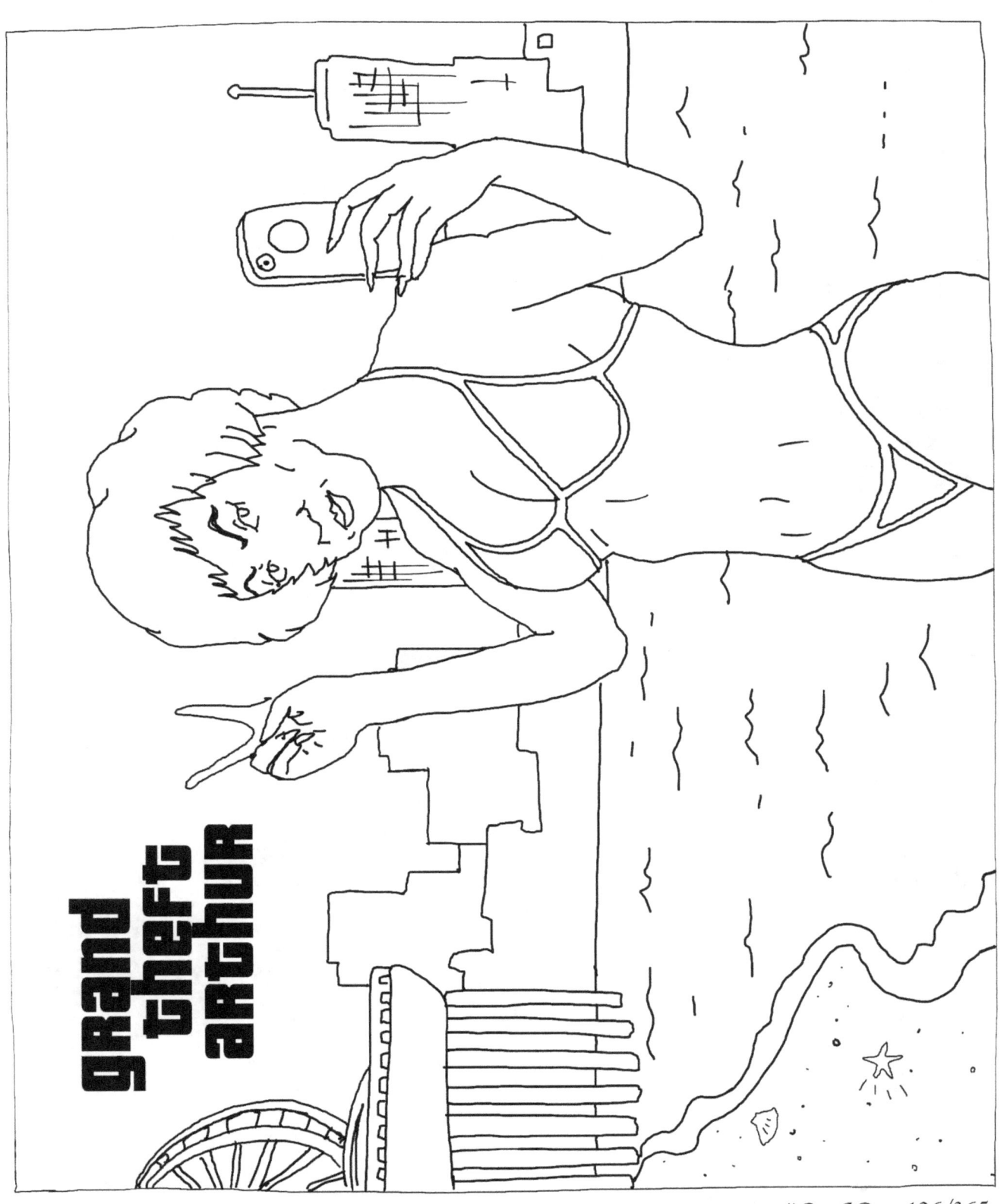

#BeaADay 126/365

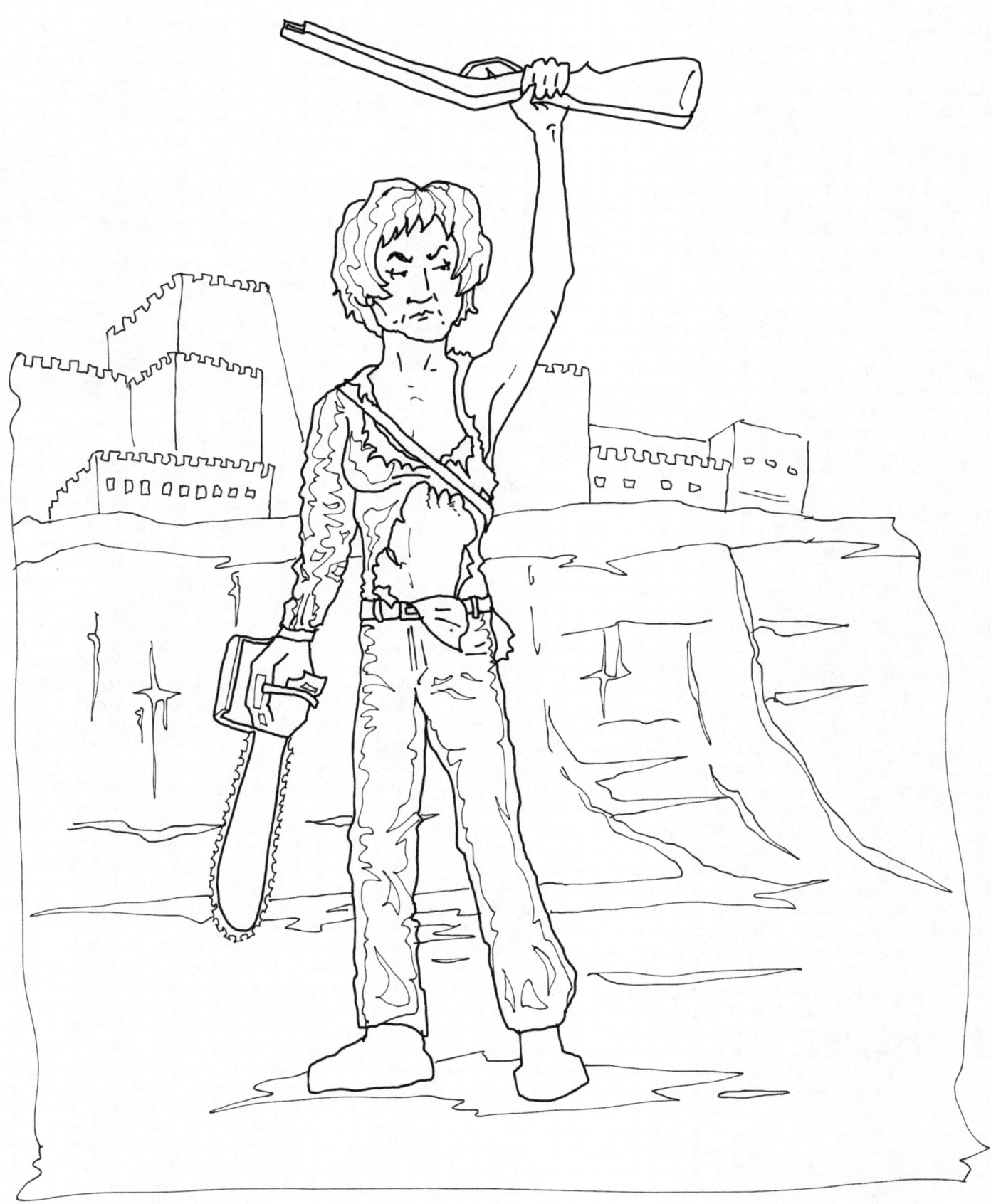

#BeaADay 129/365

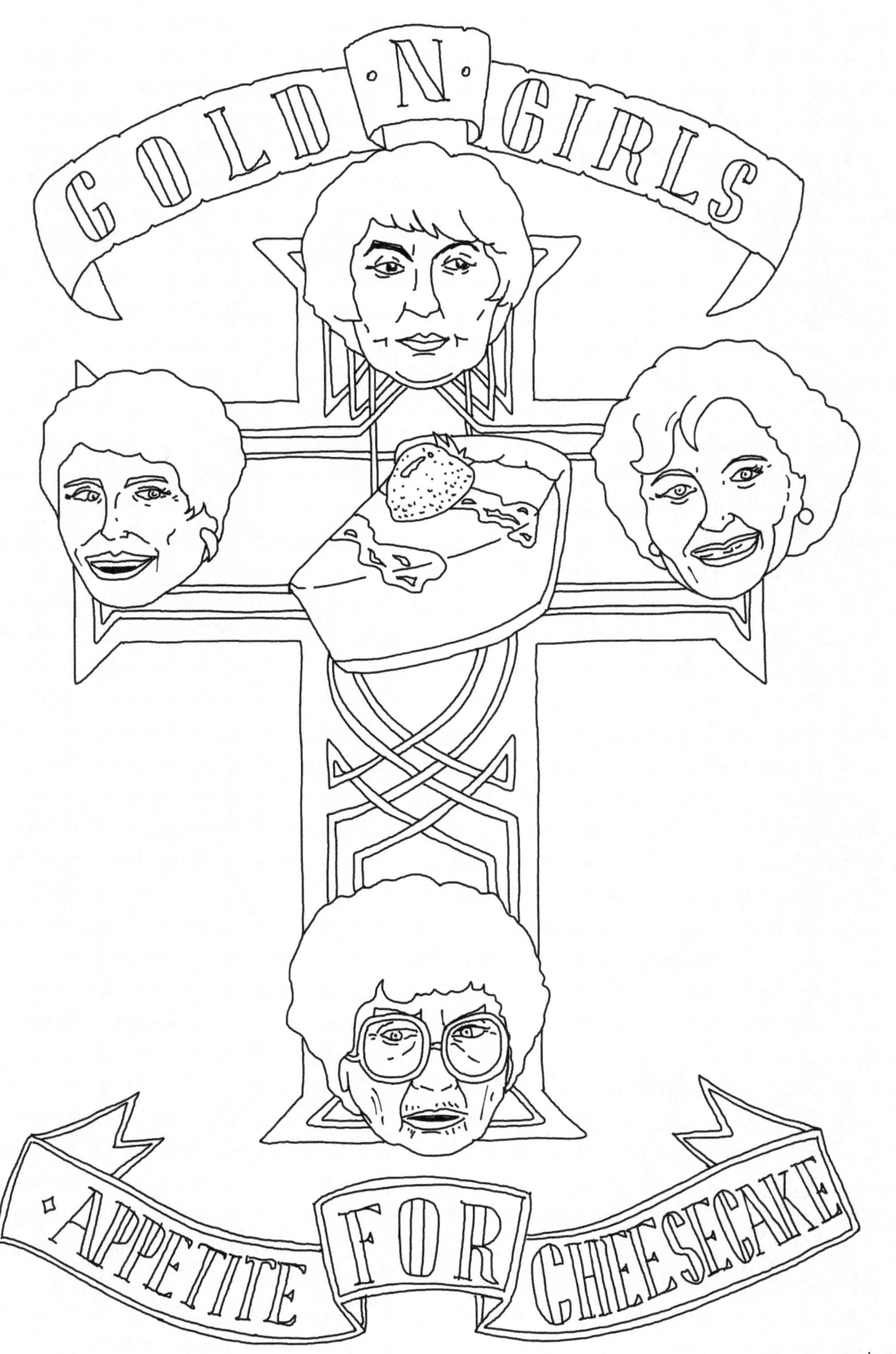

#BeaADay 157/365

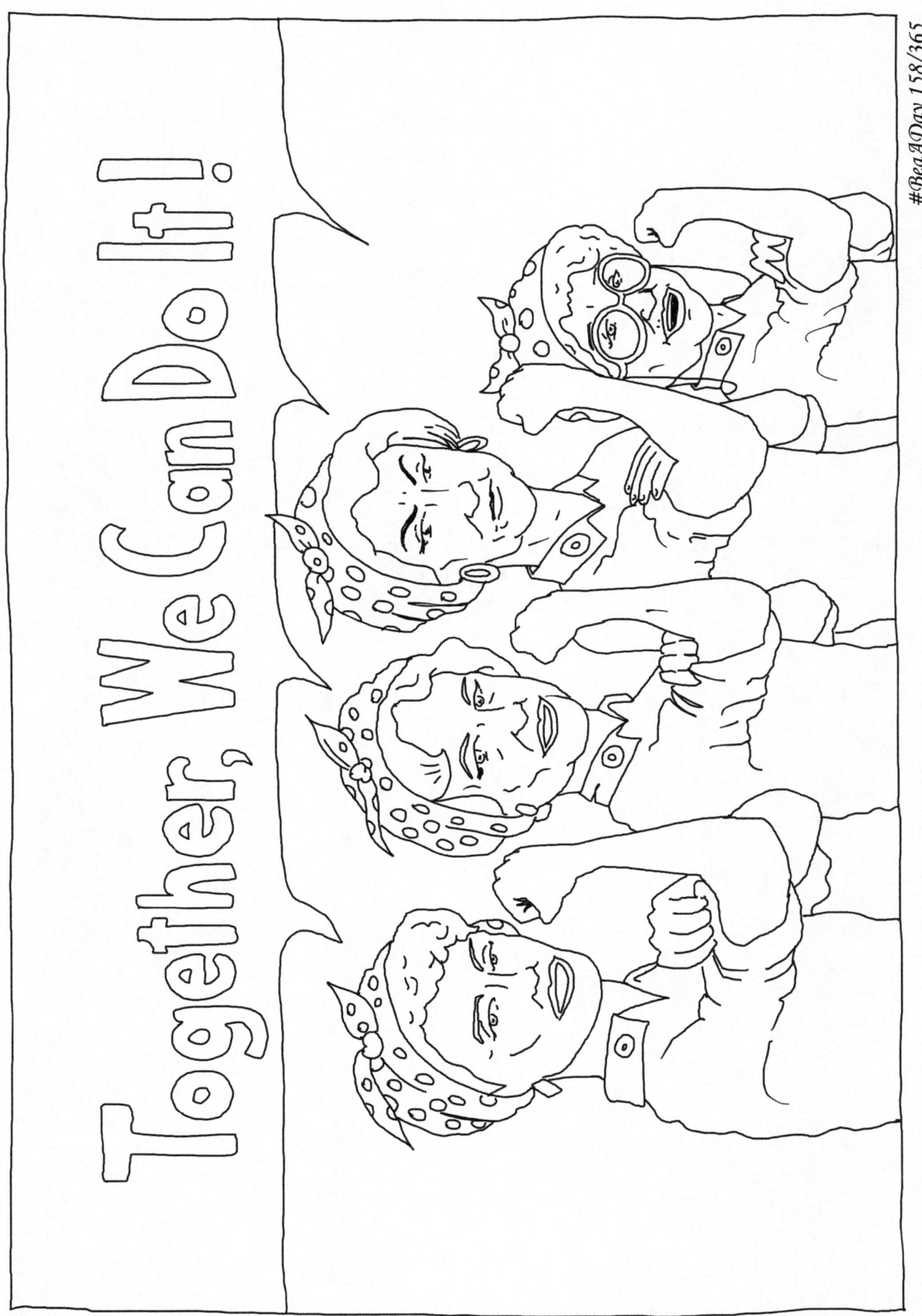

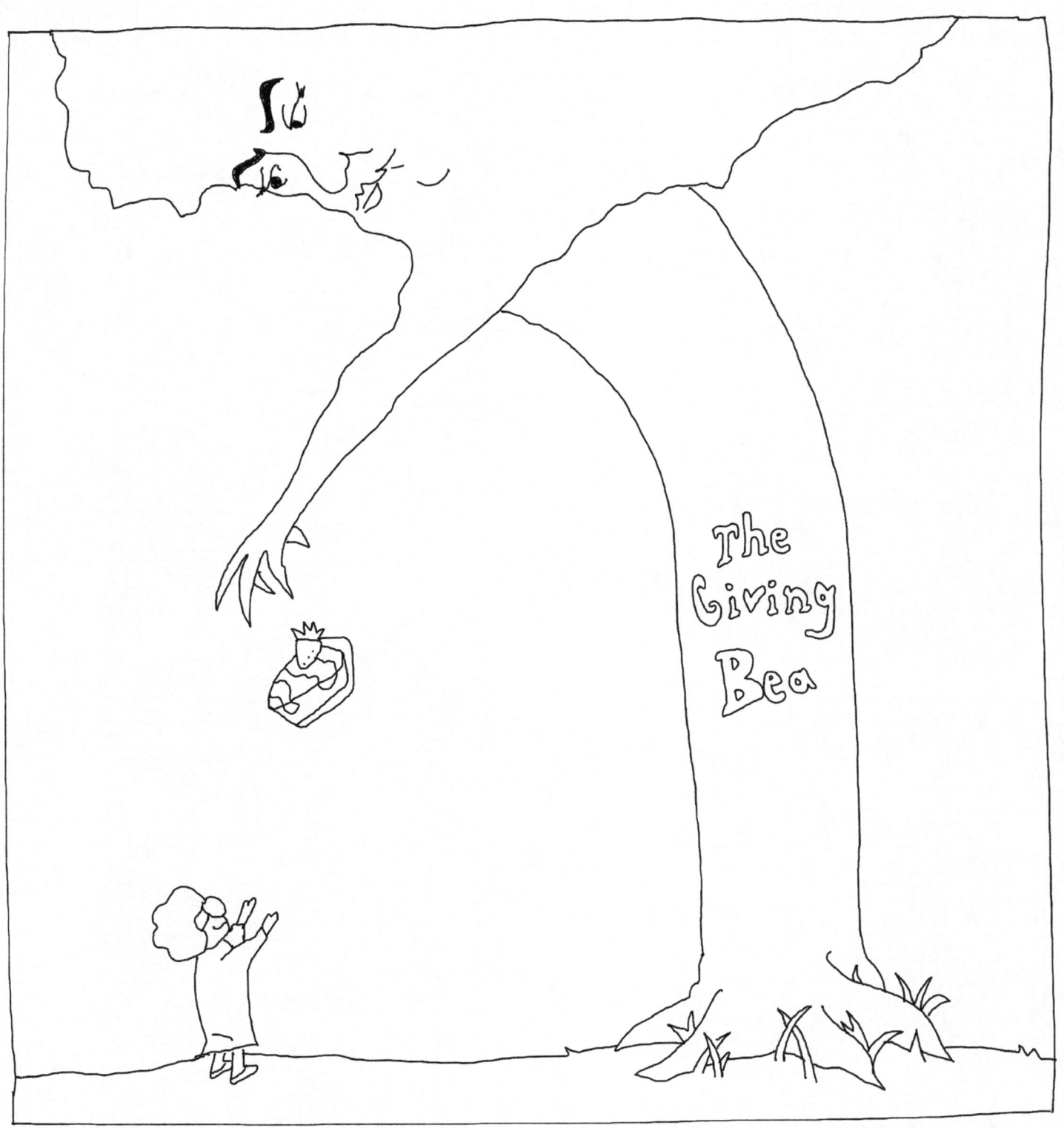

The Giving Bea

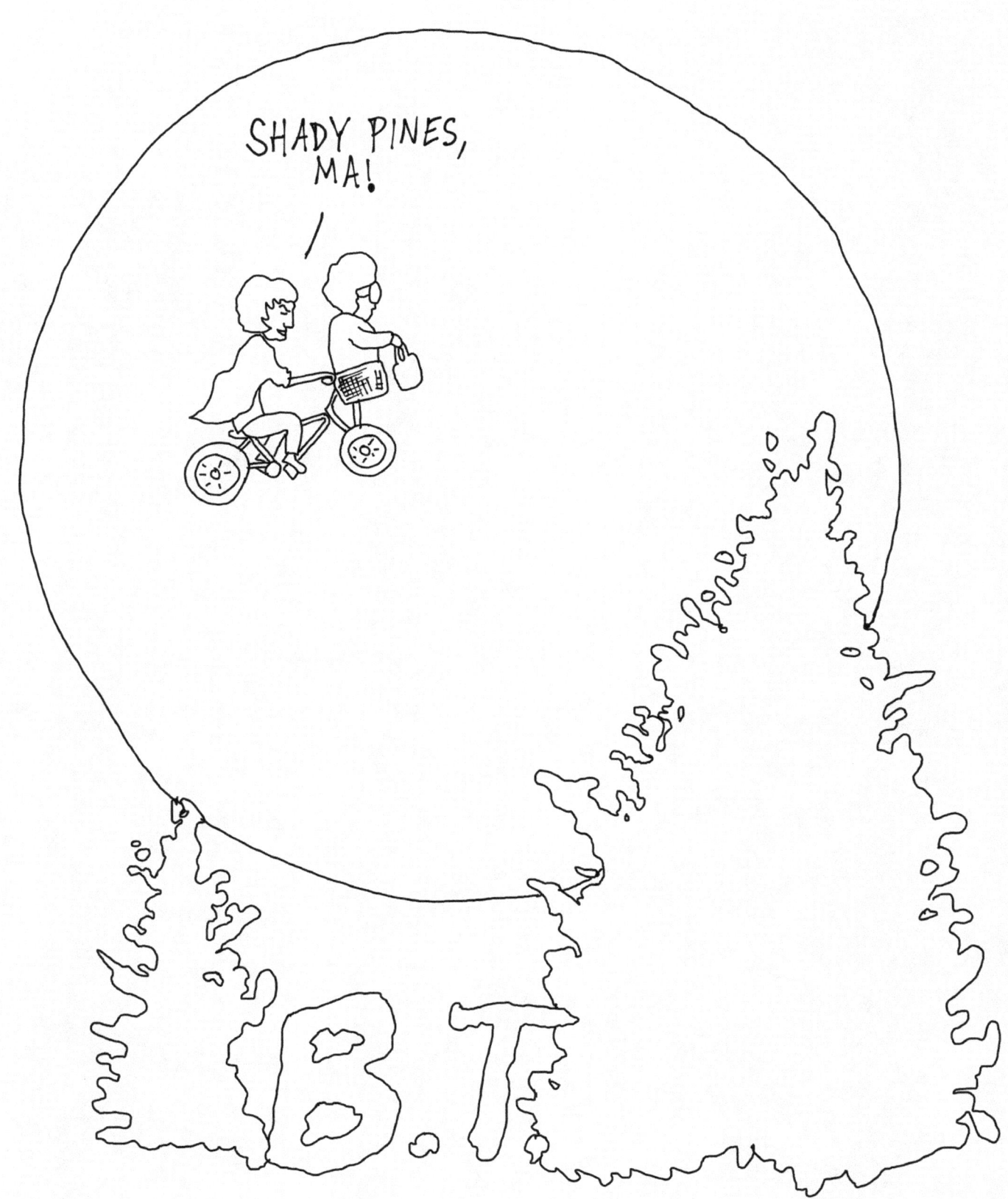

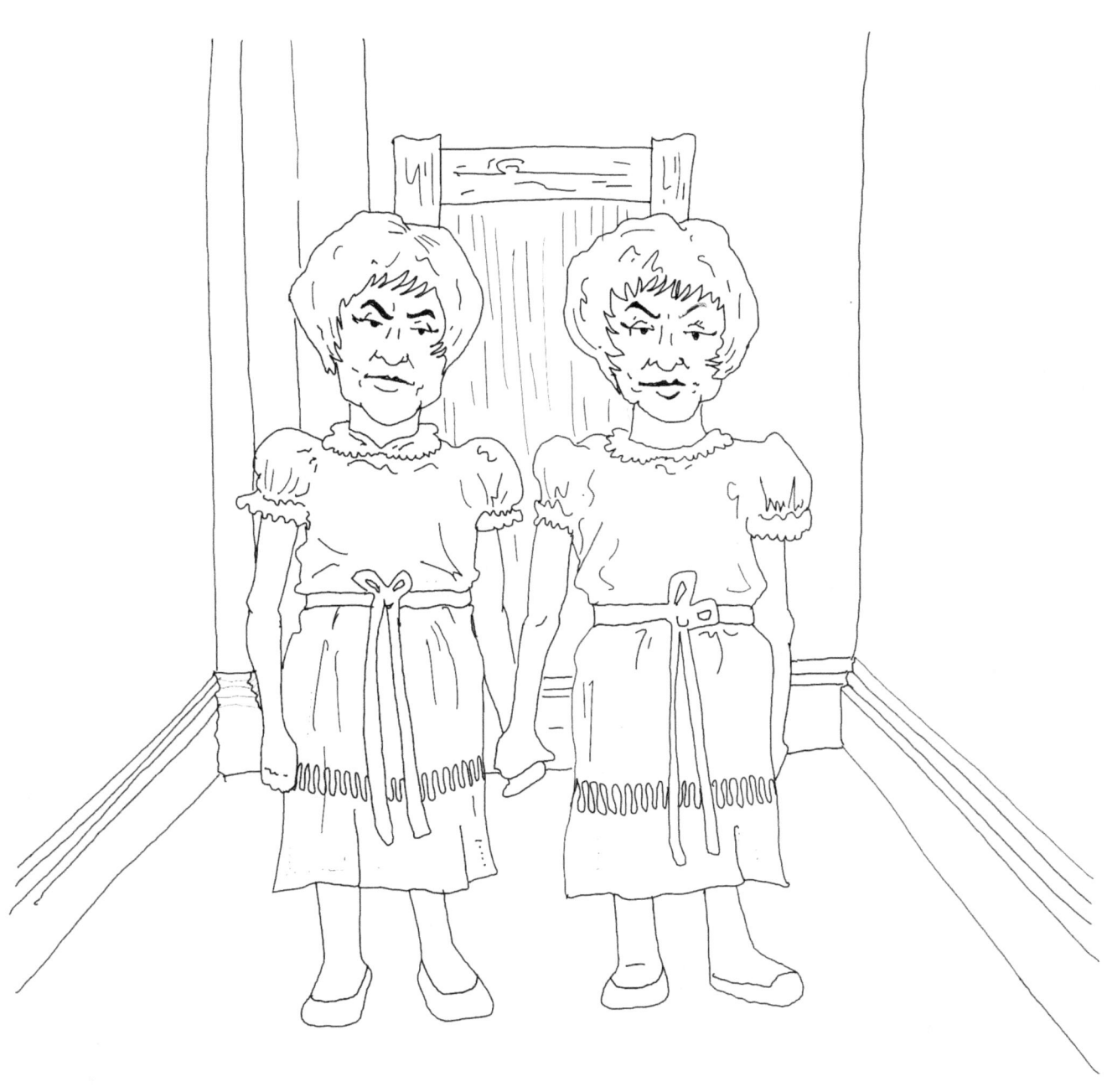

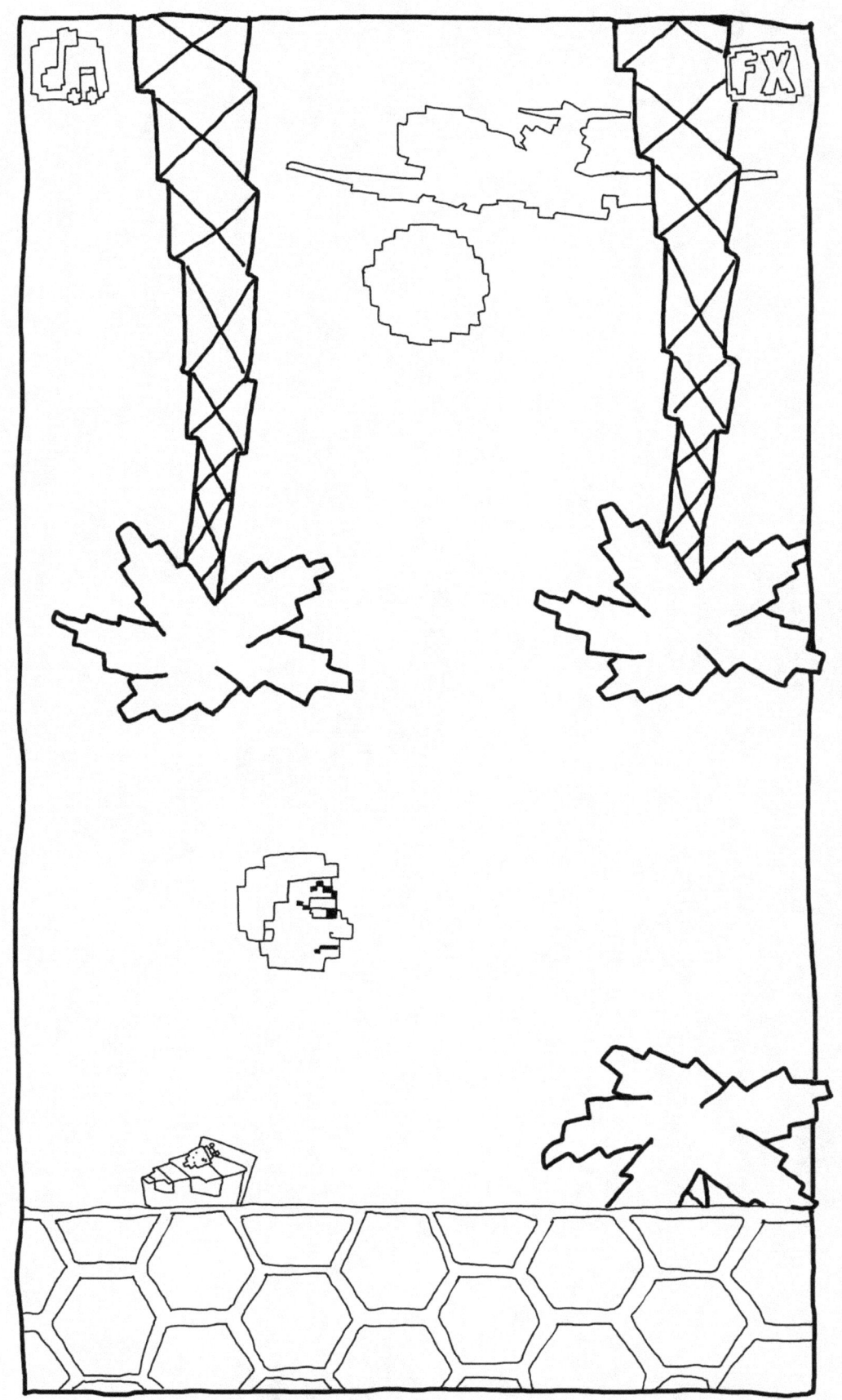

*from the Busy Bea game created by Brian Kokernak and Mike Denison
www.busybeagame.com

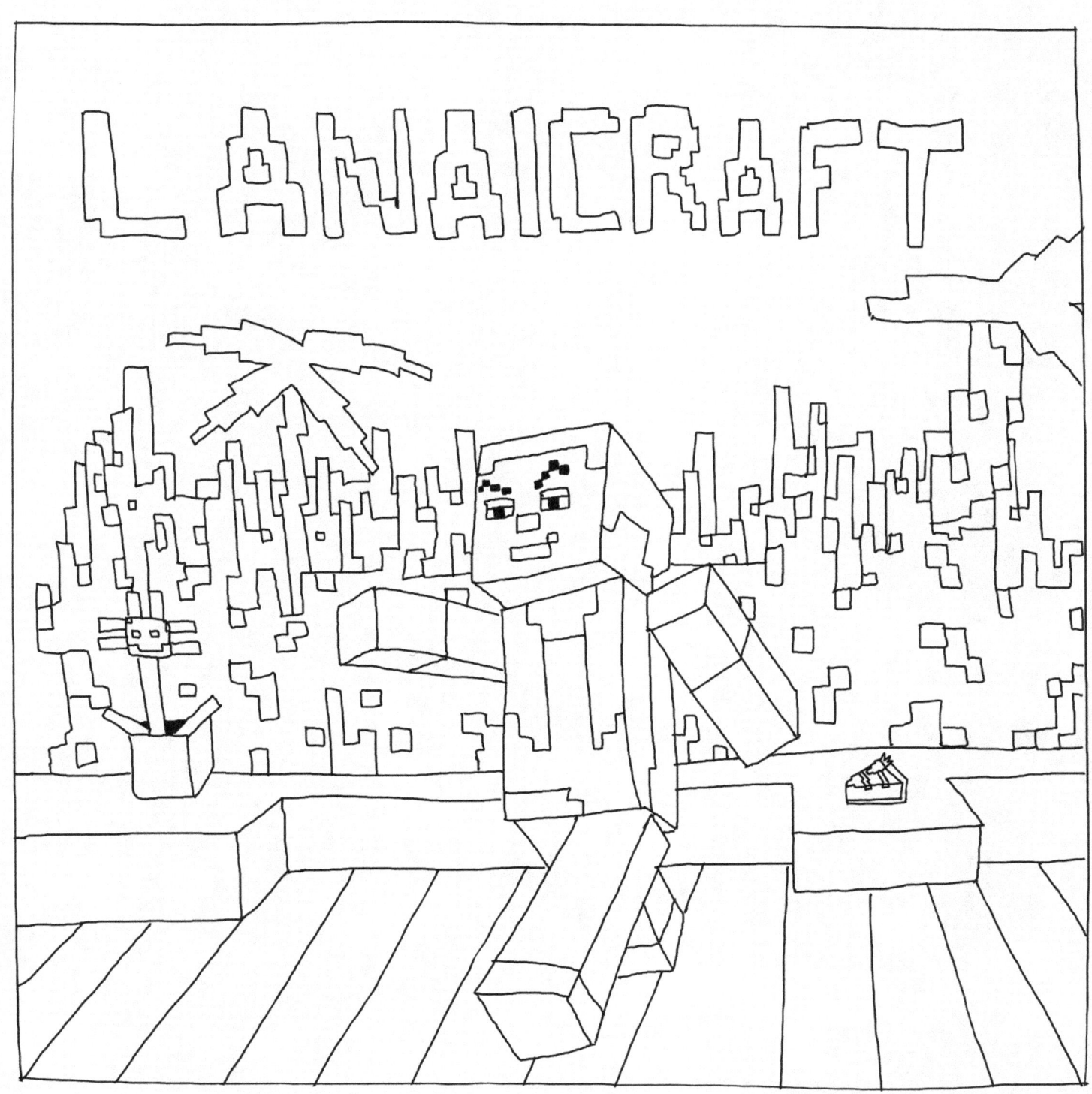

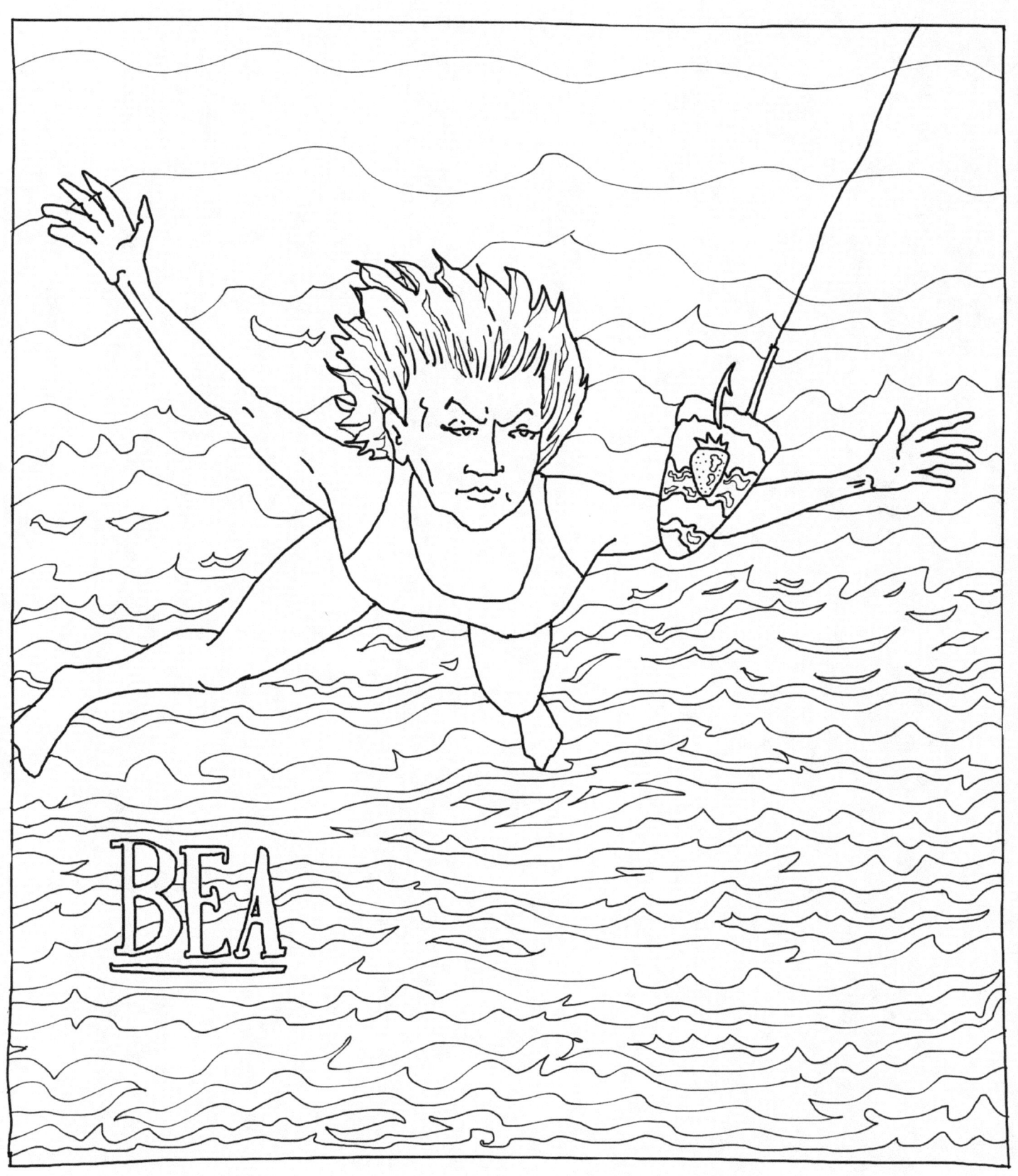

BEA

#BeaADay 211/365

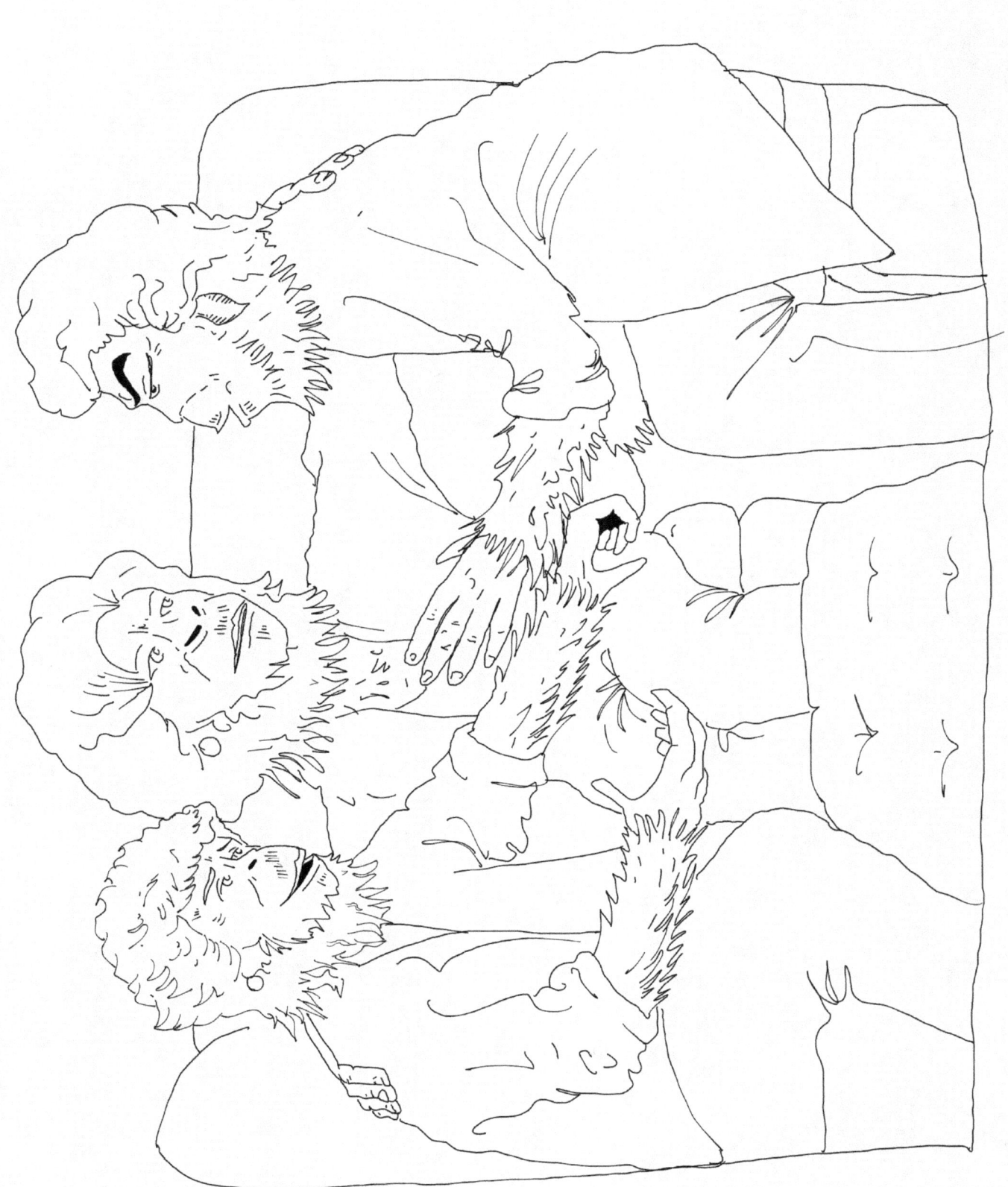

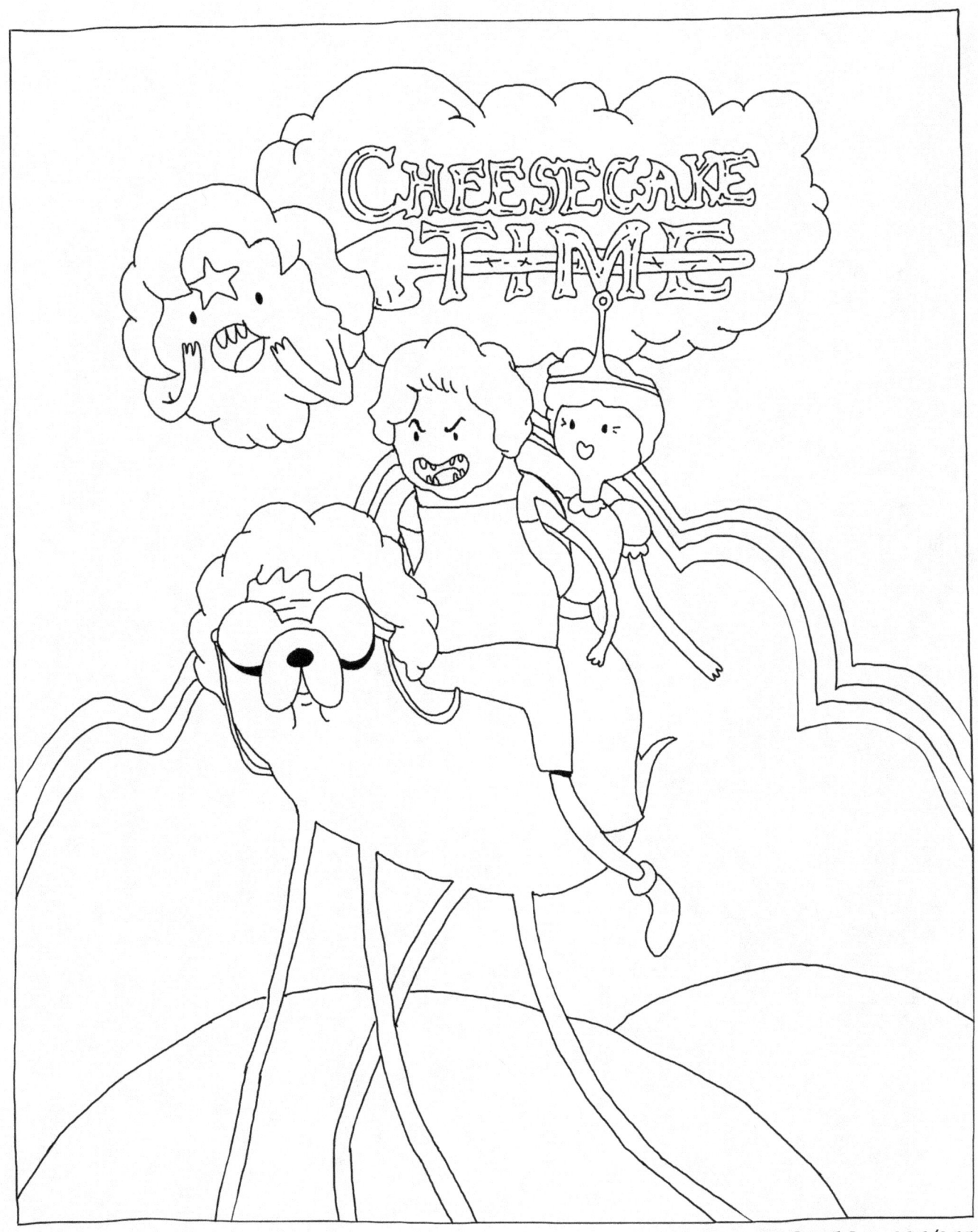

#BeaADay 336/365

BAD FOLD-IN
(BEA A DAY)

A▶ ◀

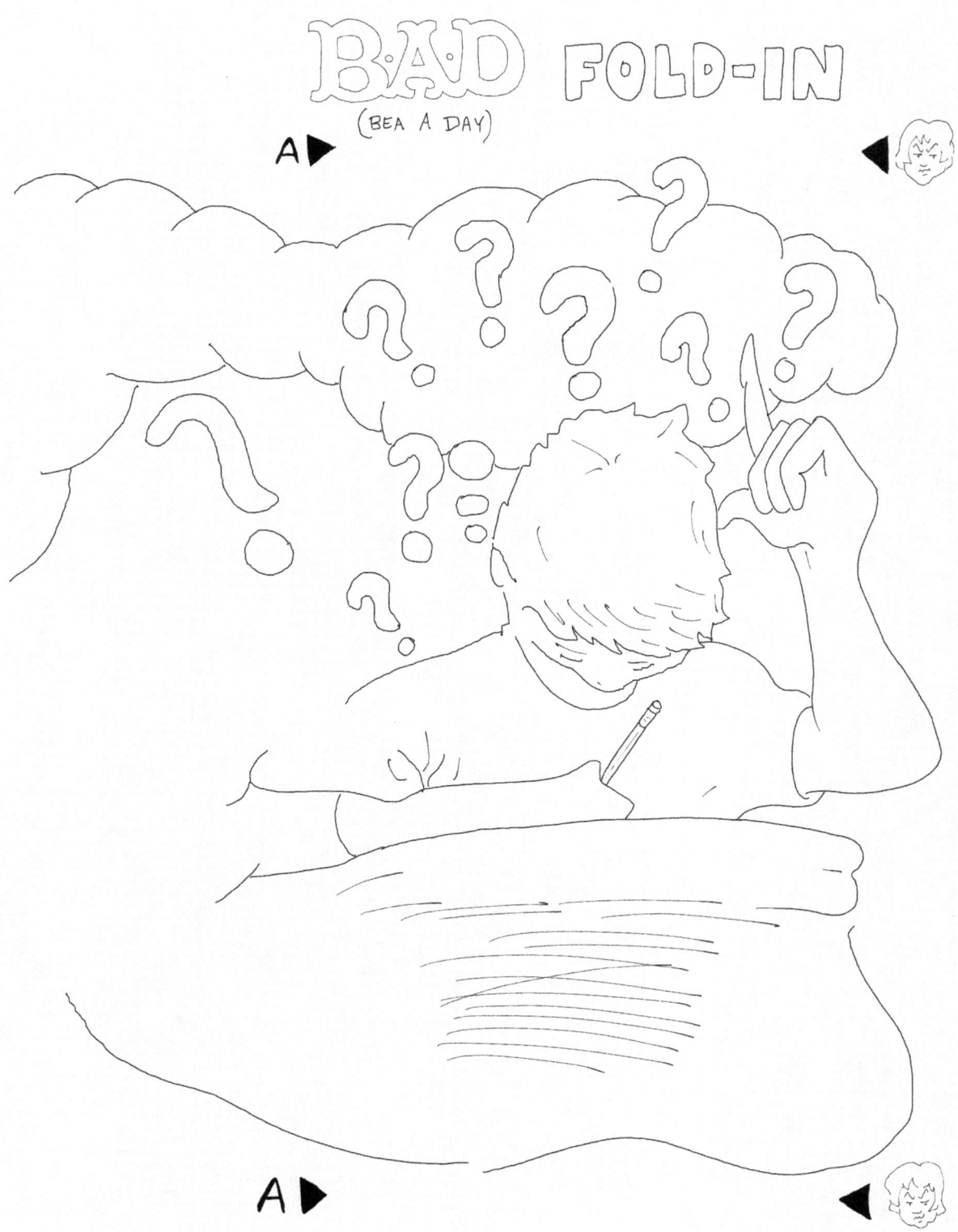

A▶ ◀

DRAW THIS FOR THE
BEST WAY TO GIVE YOURSELF A
CREATIVE CHALLENGE.

*Fold the page matching the A arrows to the Bea arrows
to reveal the image*

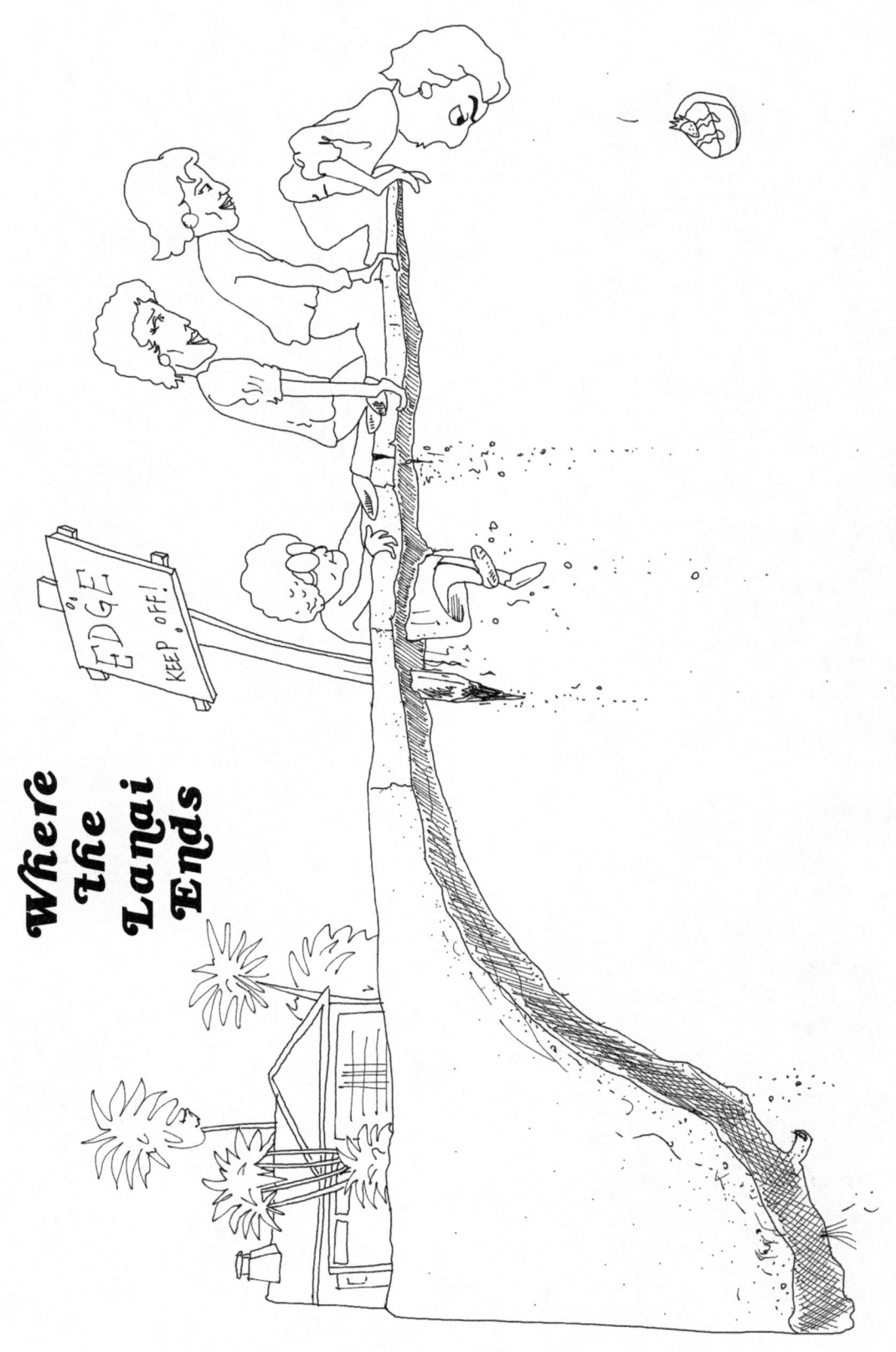

2. #BettyADay

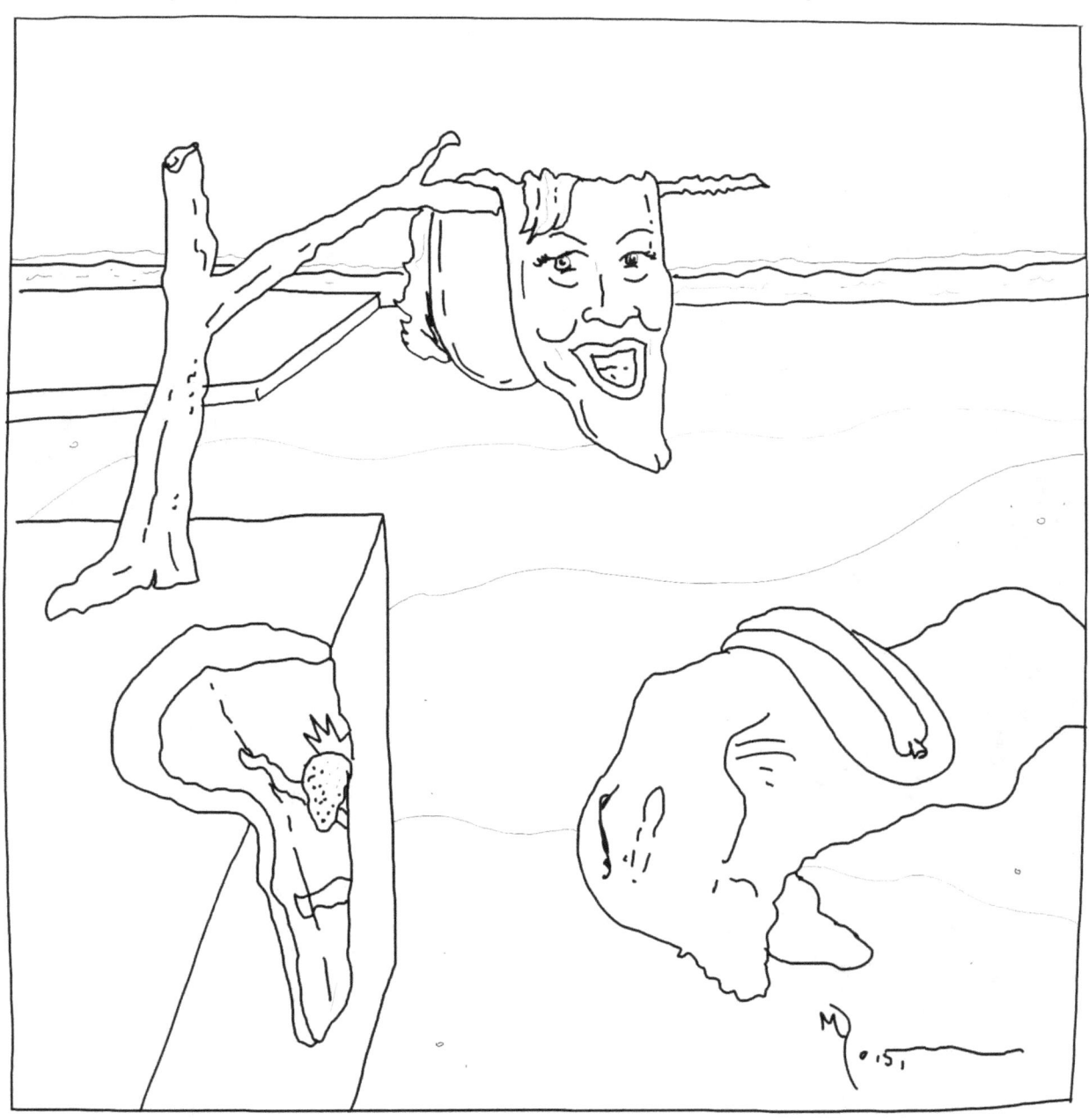

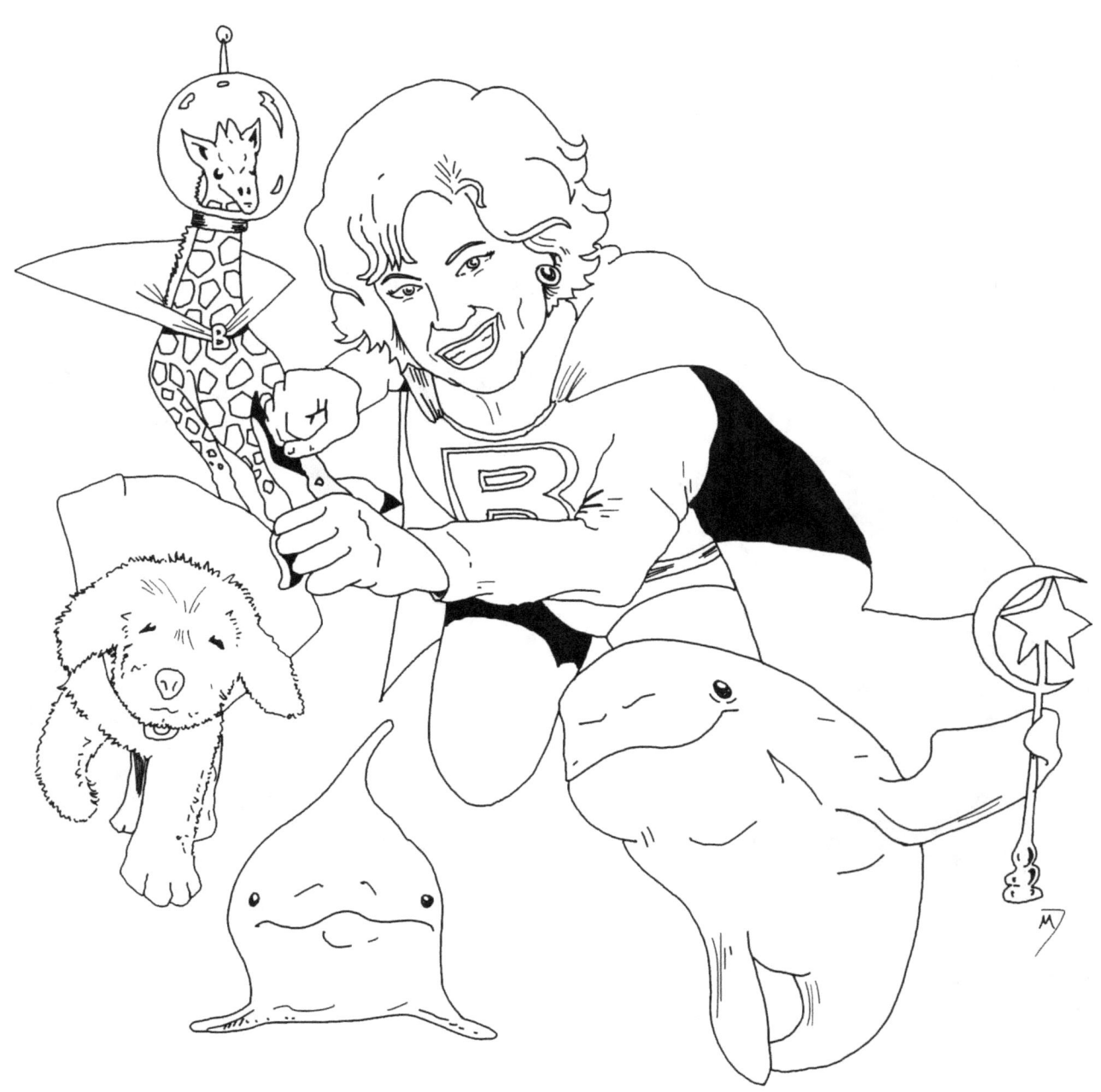

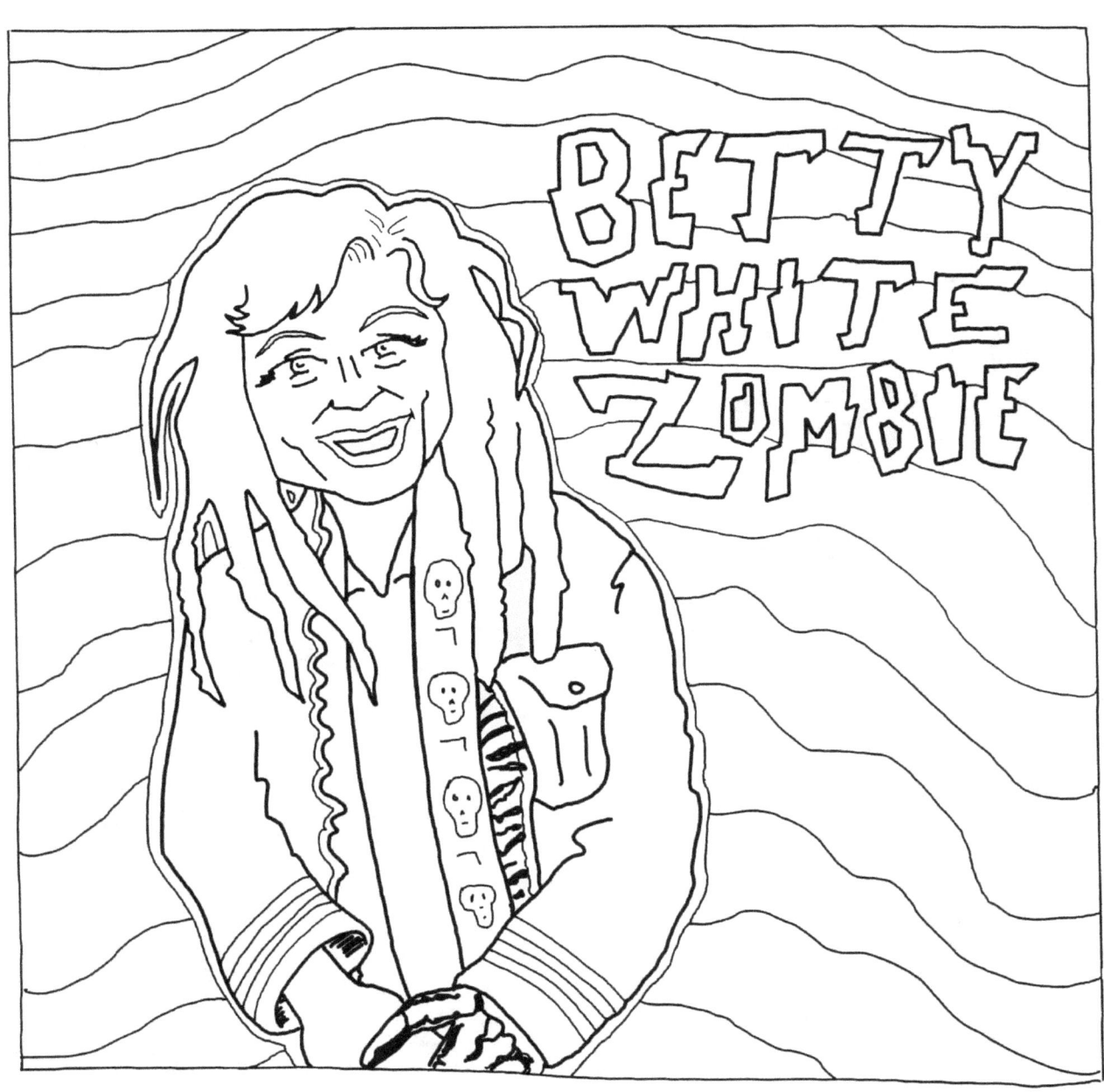

#BettyADay 10/365

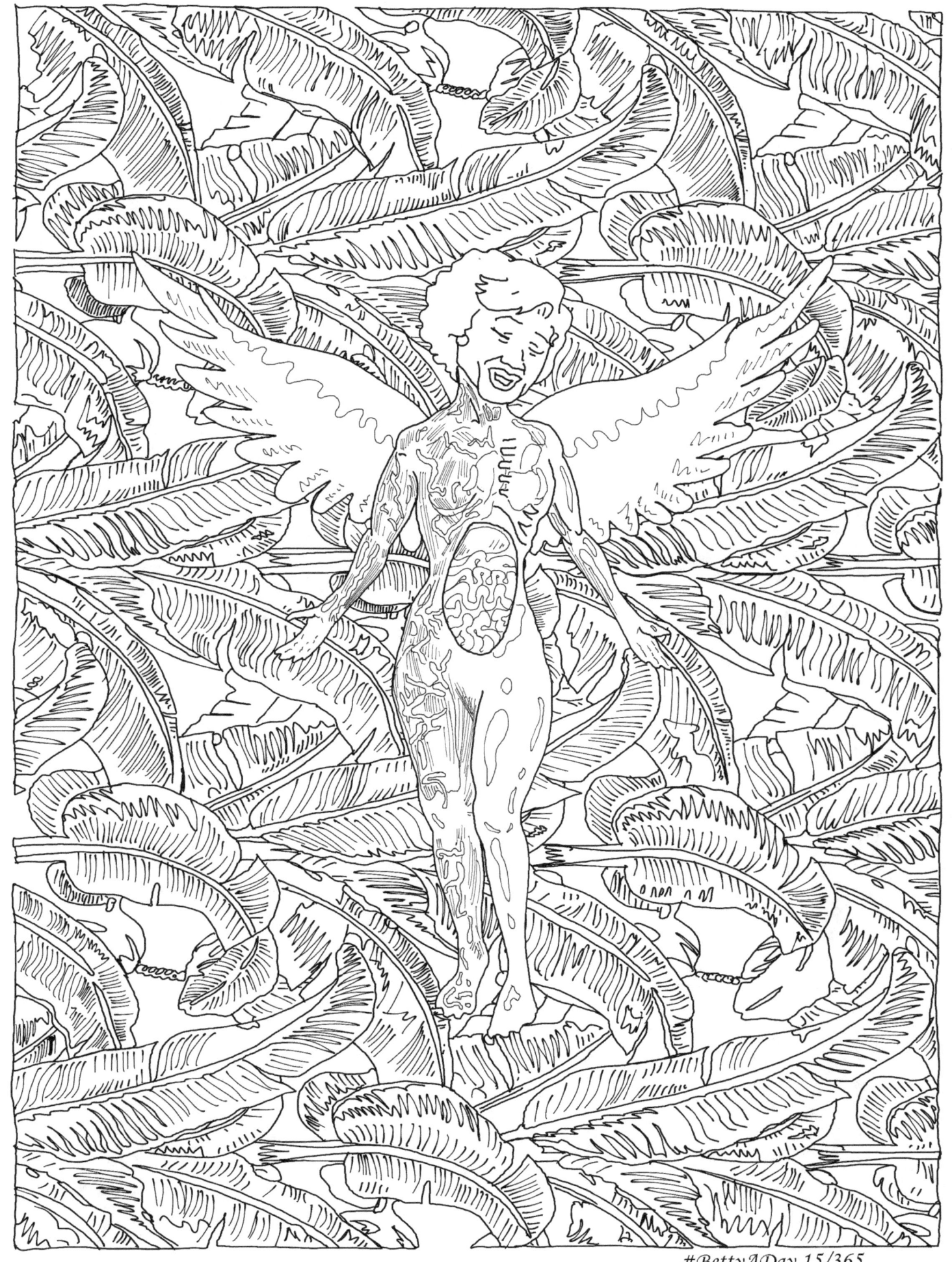

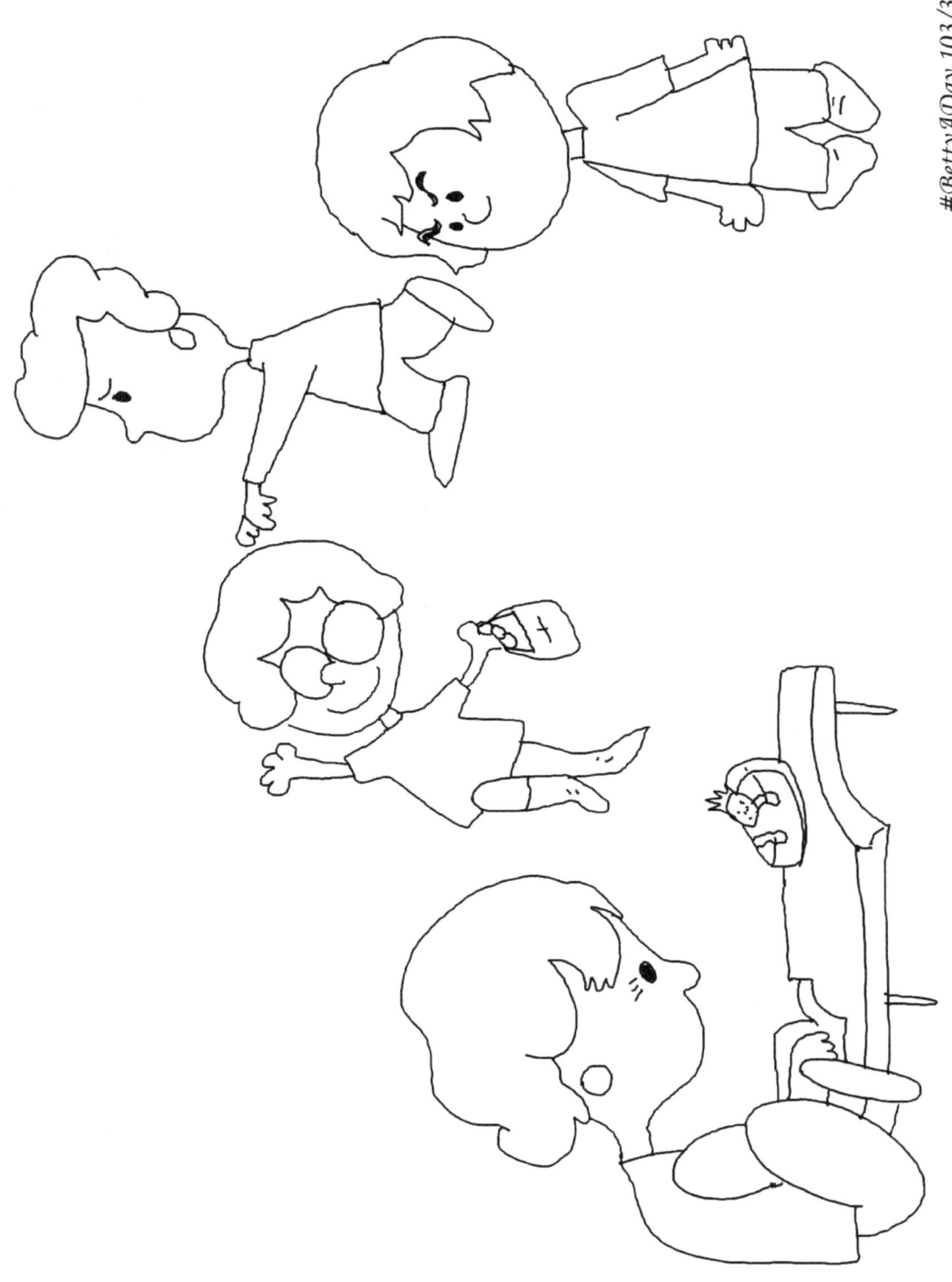

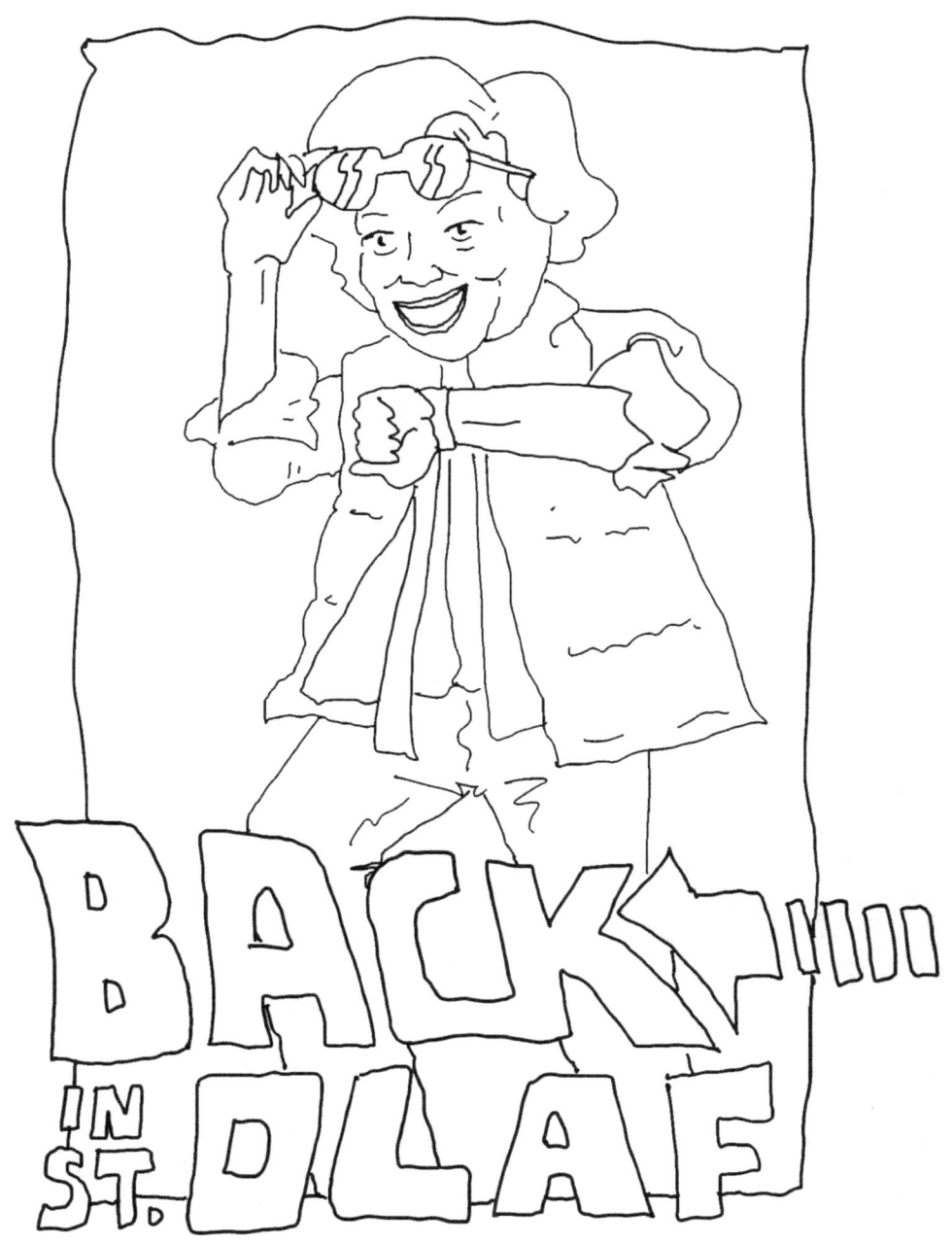

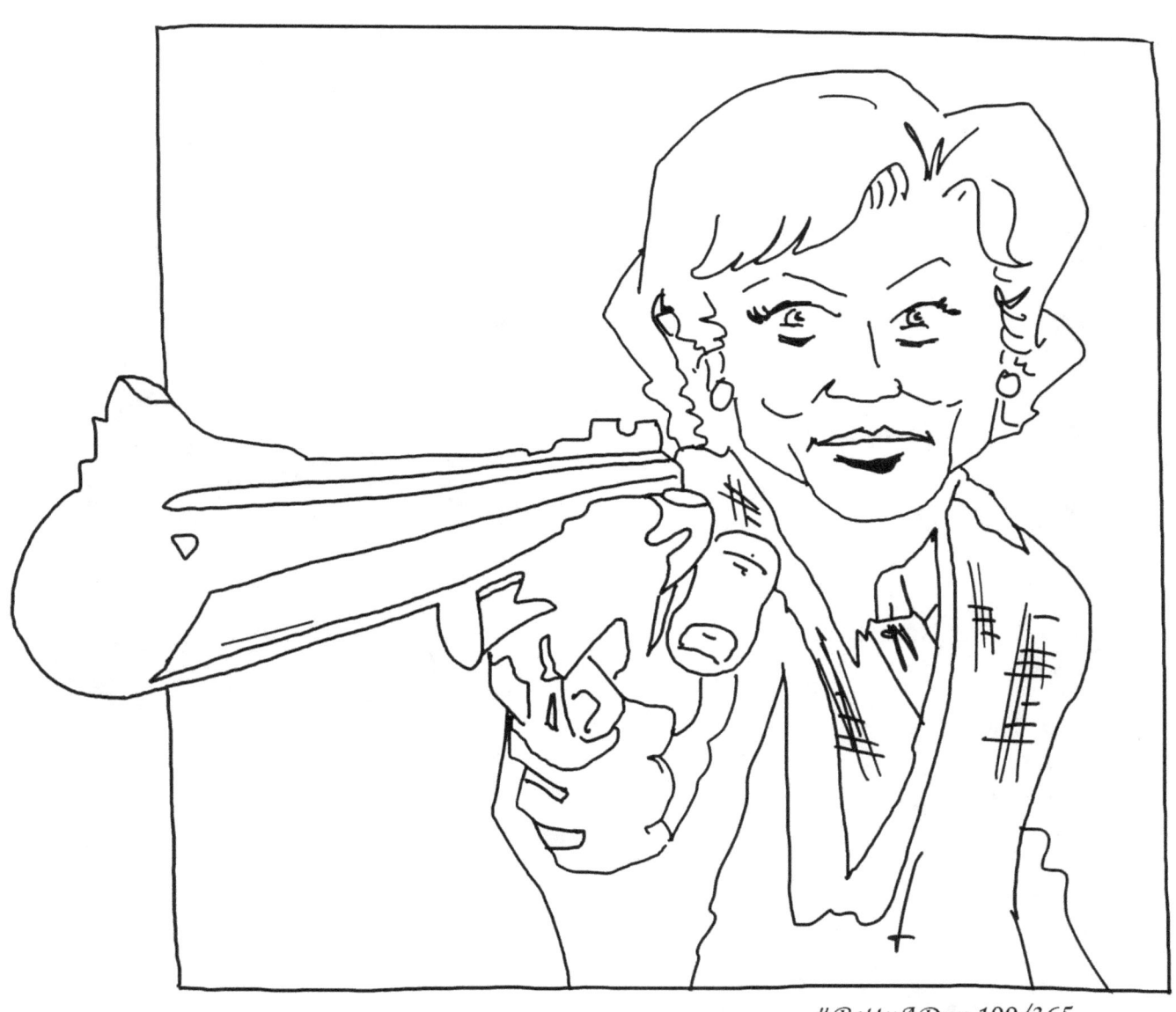

#BettyADay 199/365

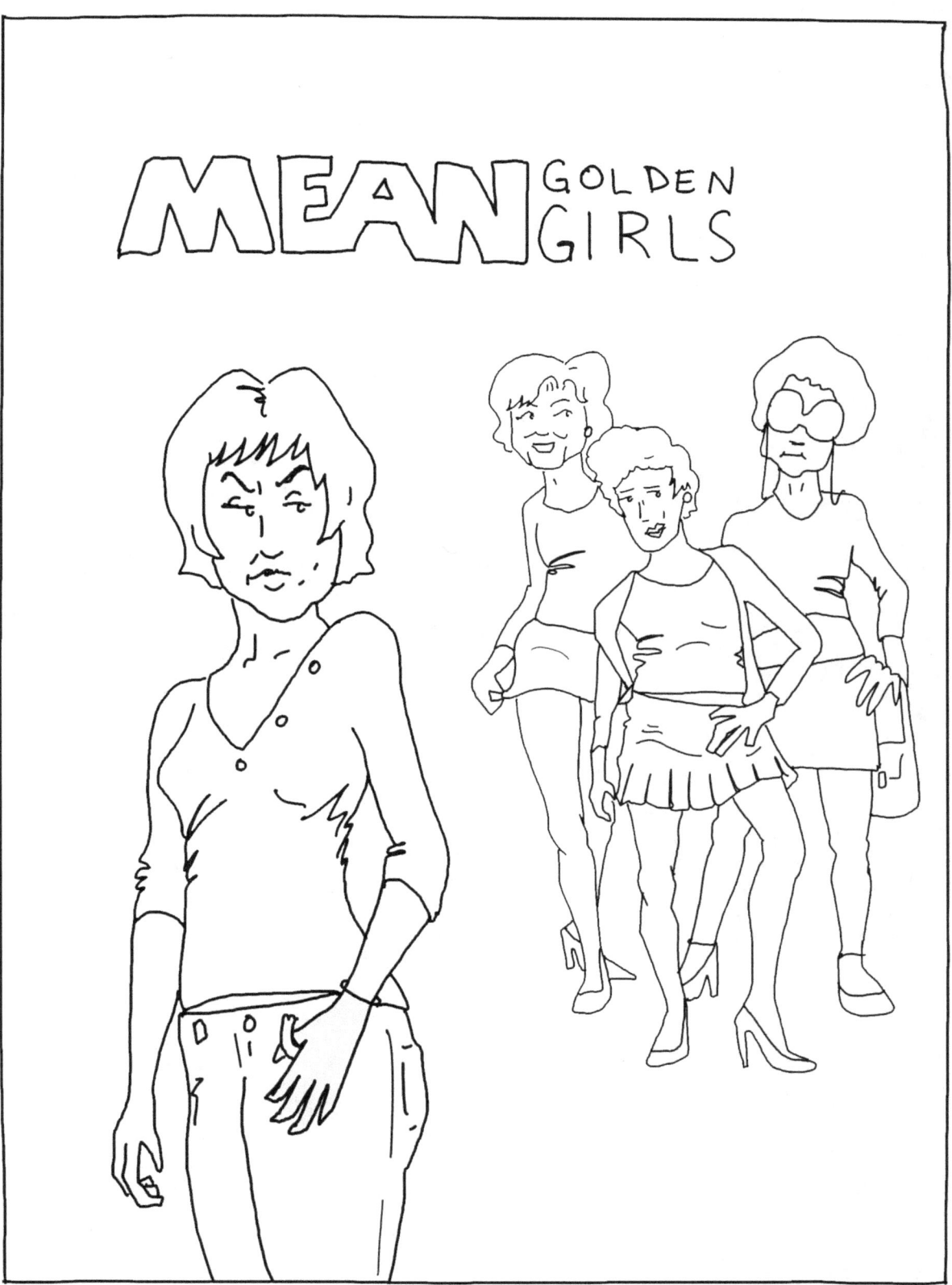

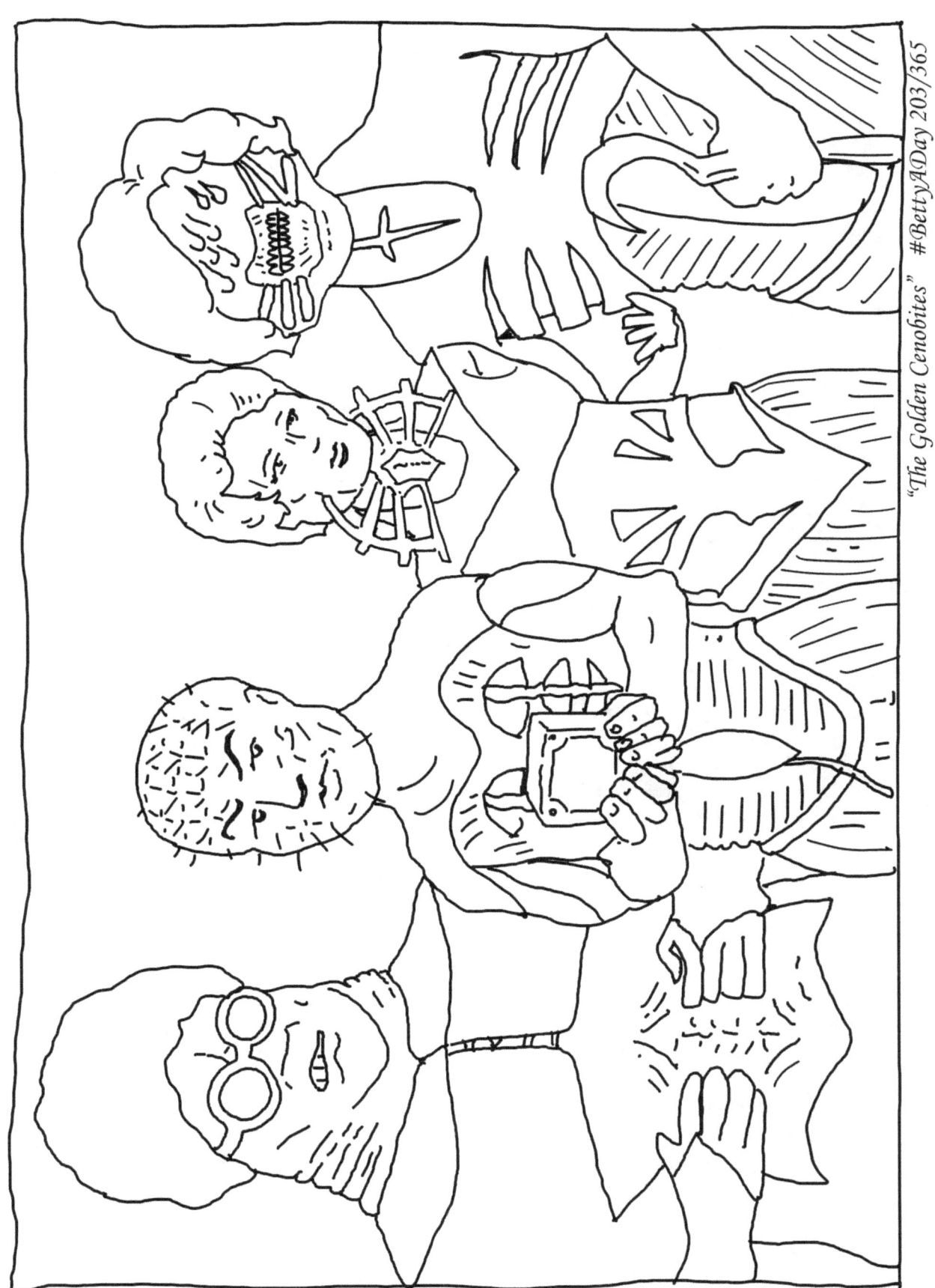

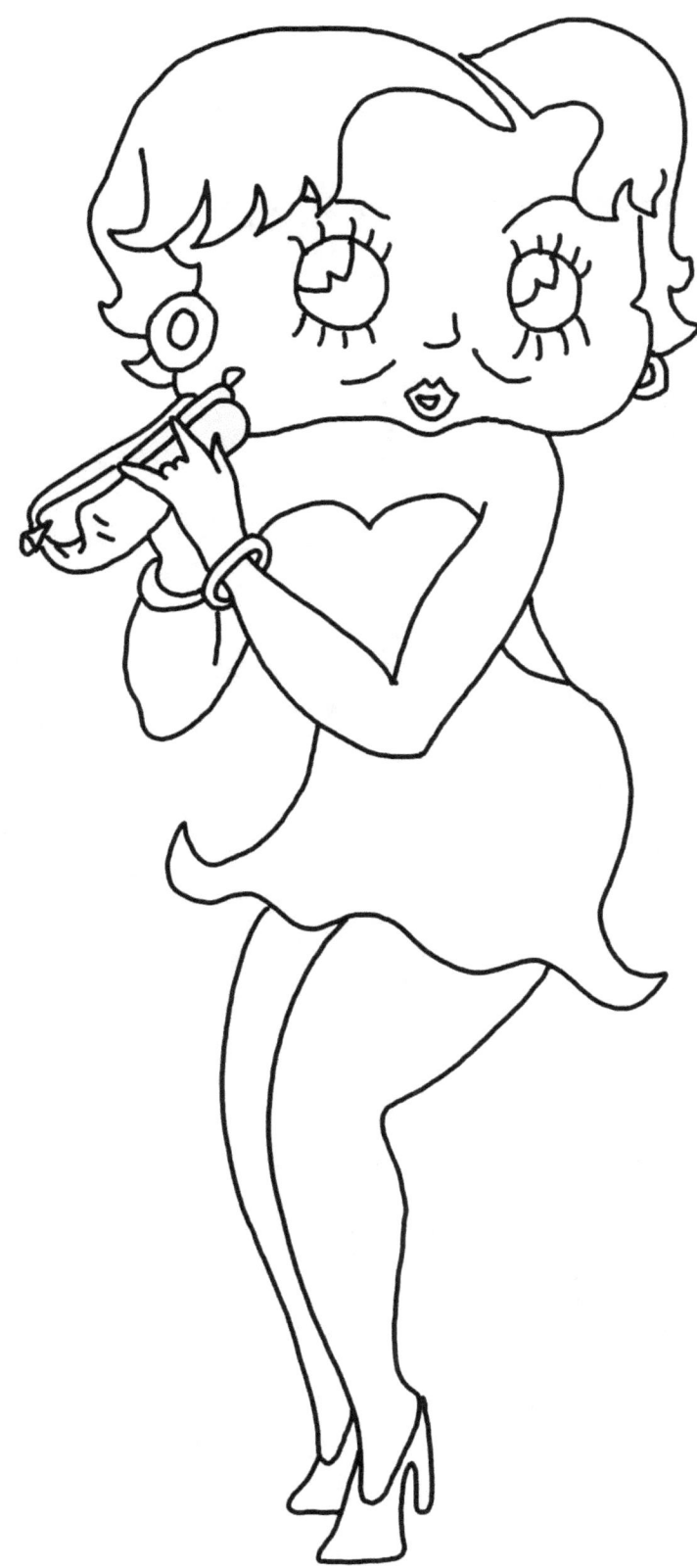

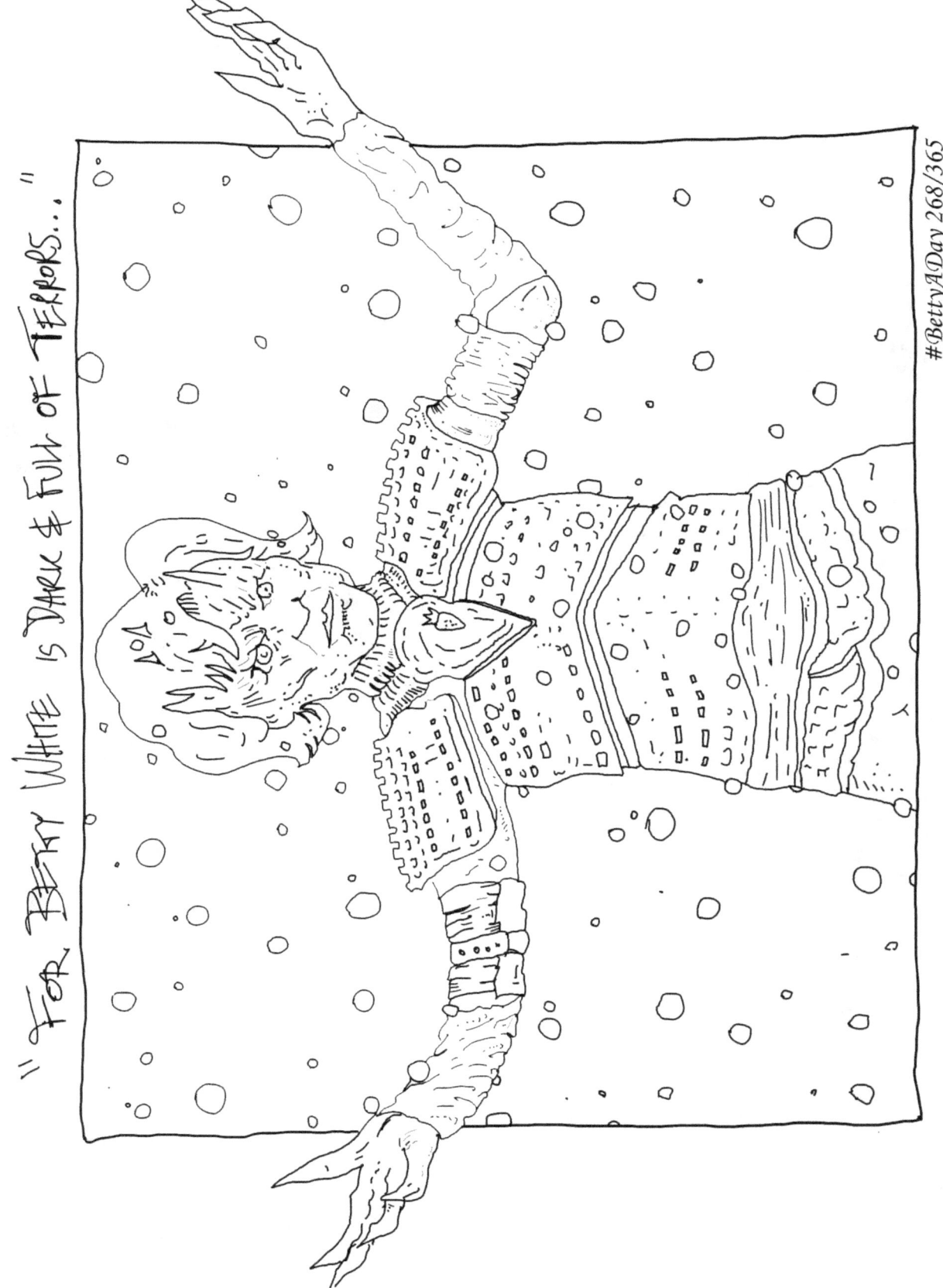

"For Betty White is Dark & Full of Terrors..."

#BettyADay 268/365

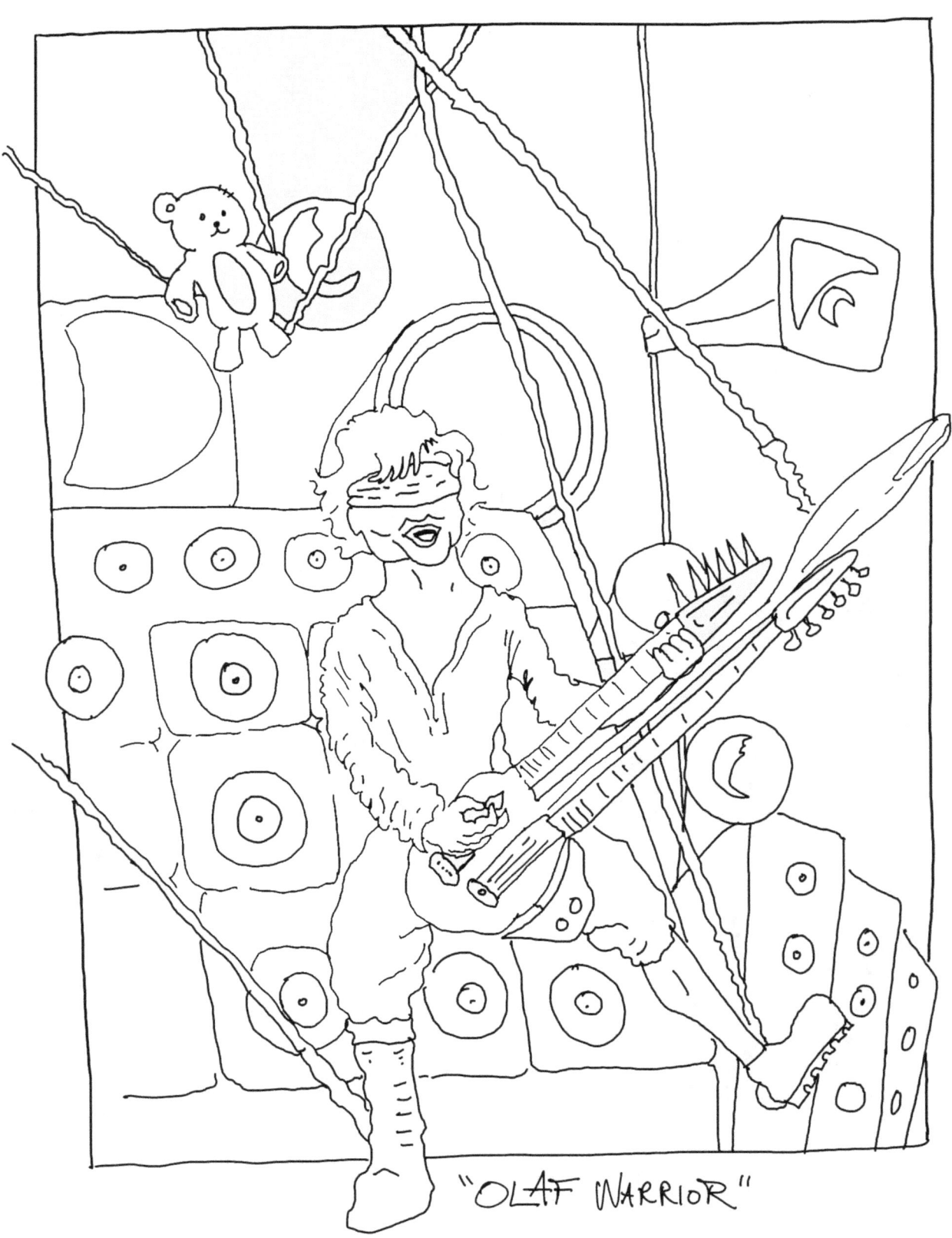

"OLAF WARRIOR"

3. #RueTheDay

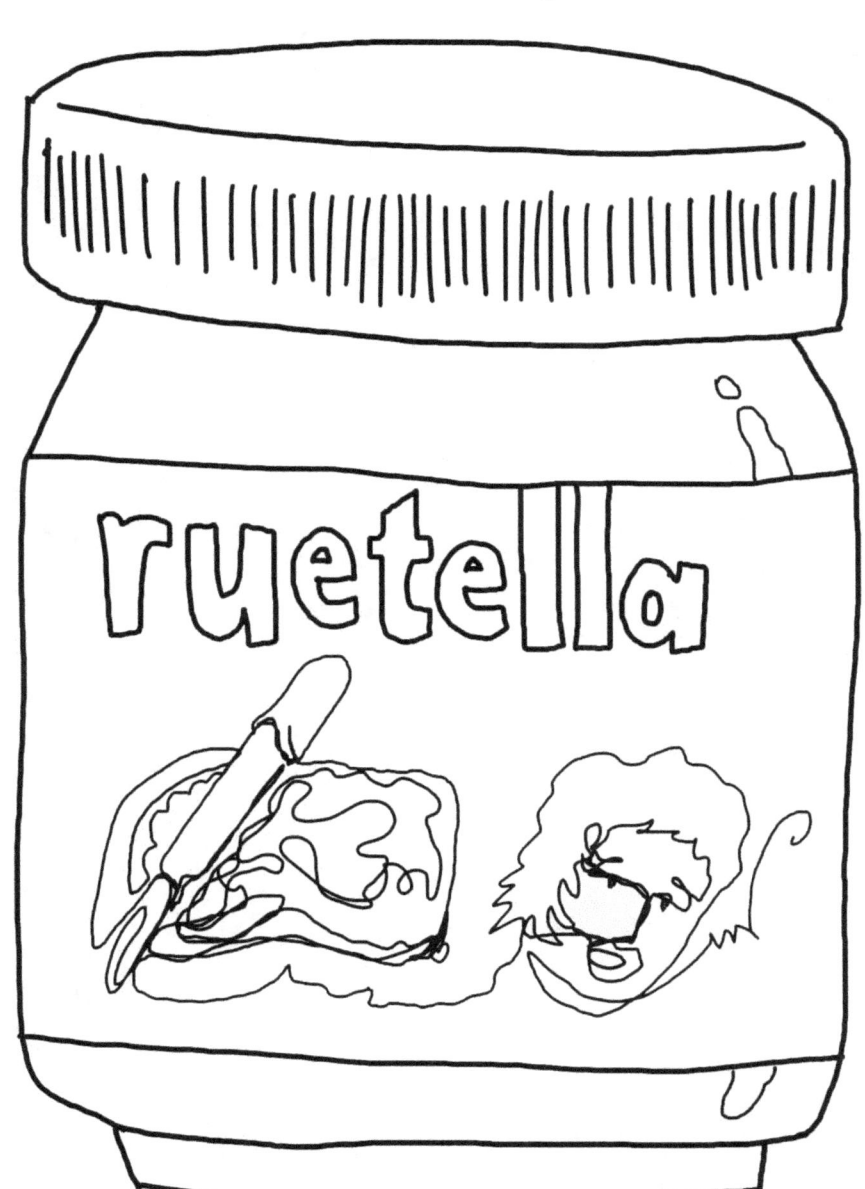

By Dr. Ruess

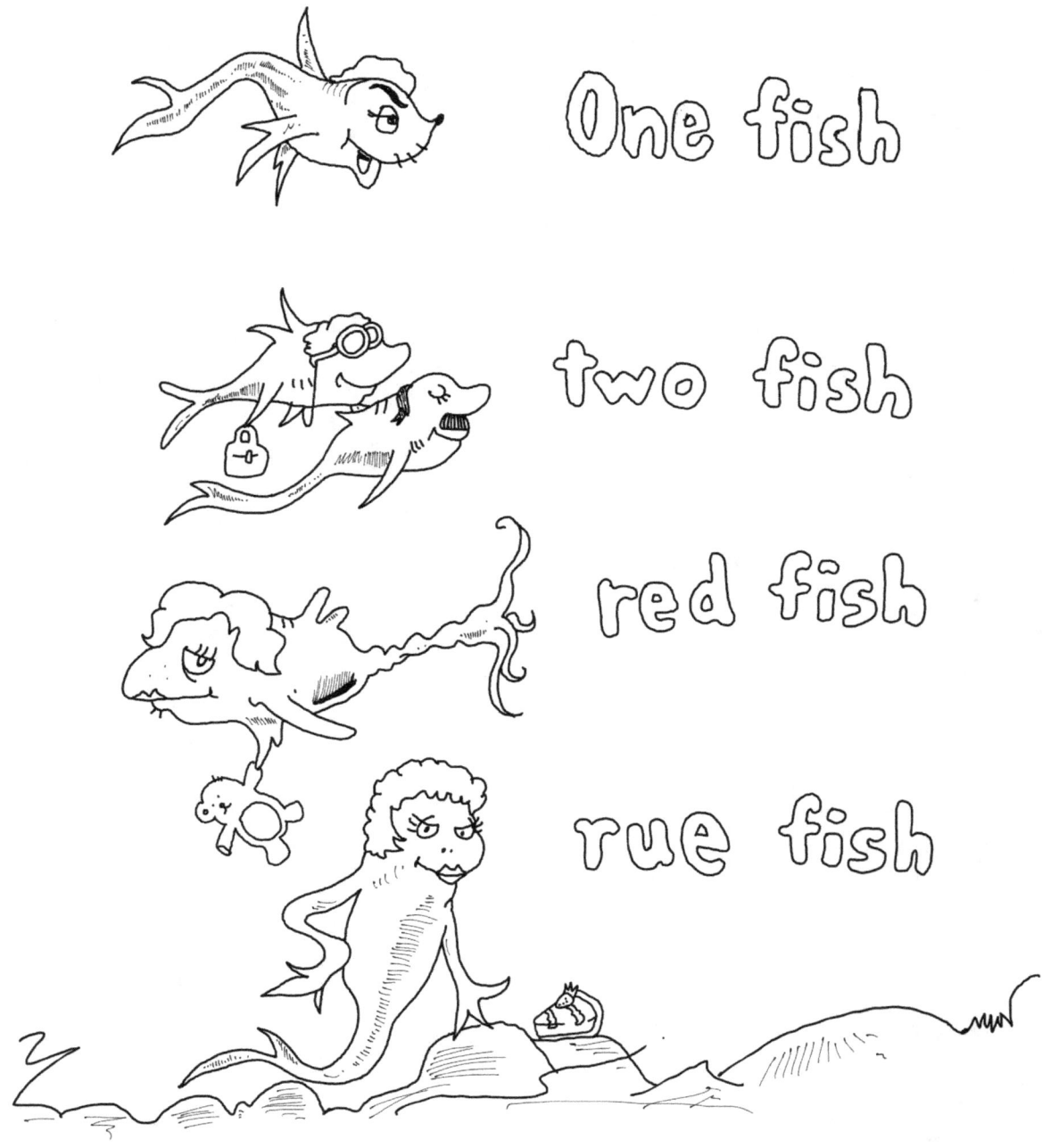

One fish

two fish

red fish

rue fish

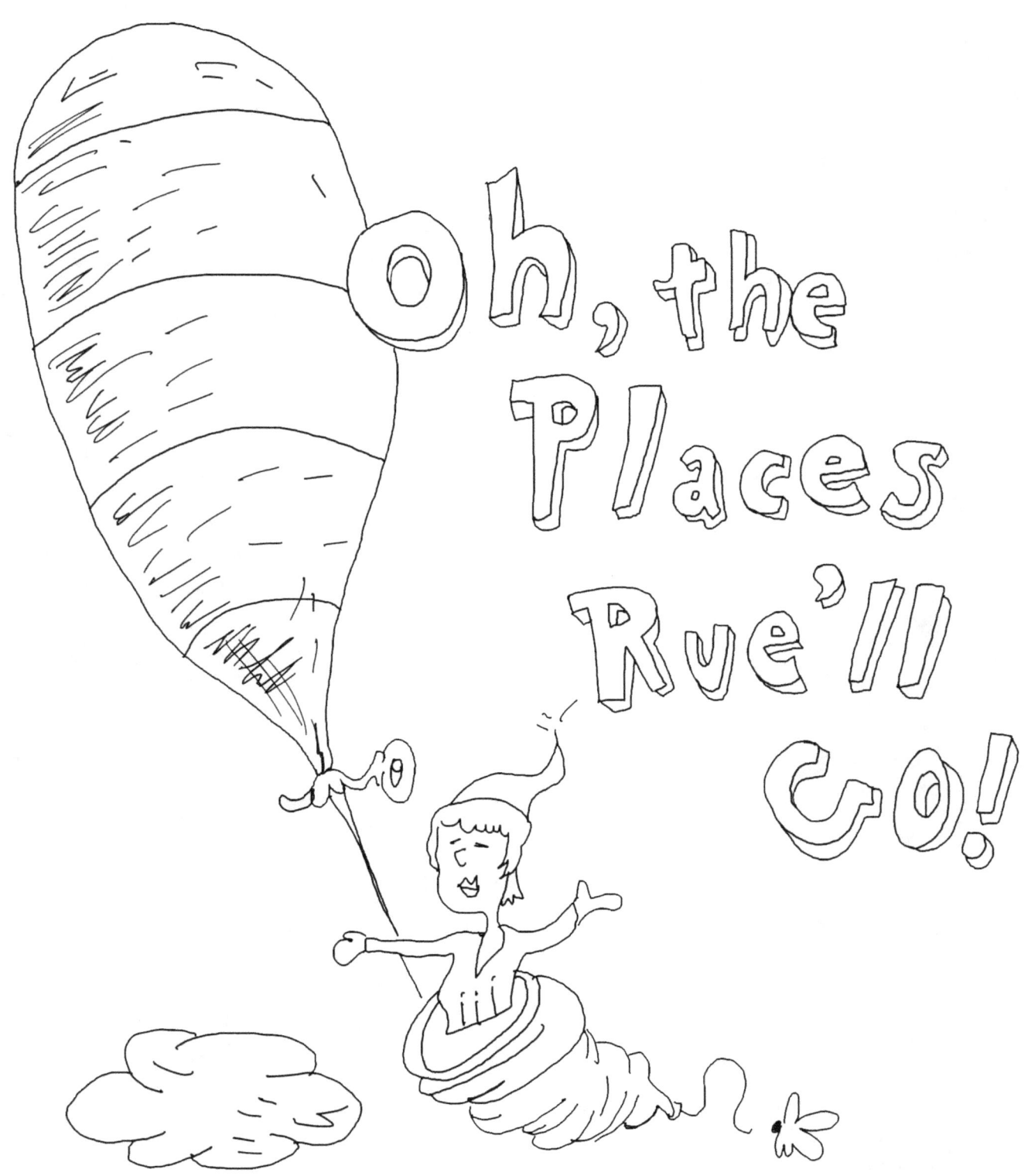

Oh, the Places Rue'll Go!

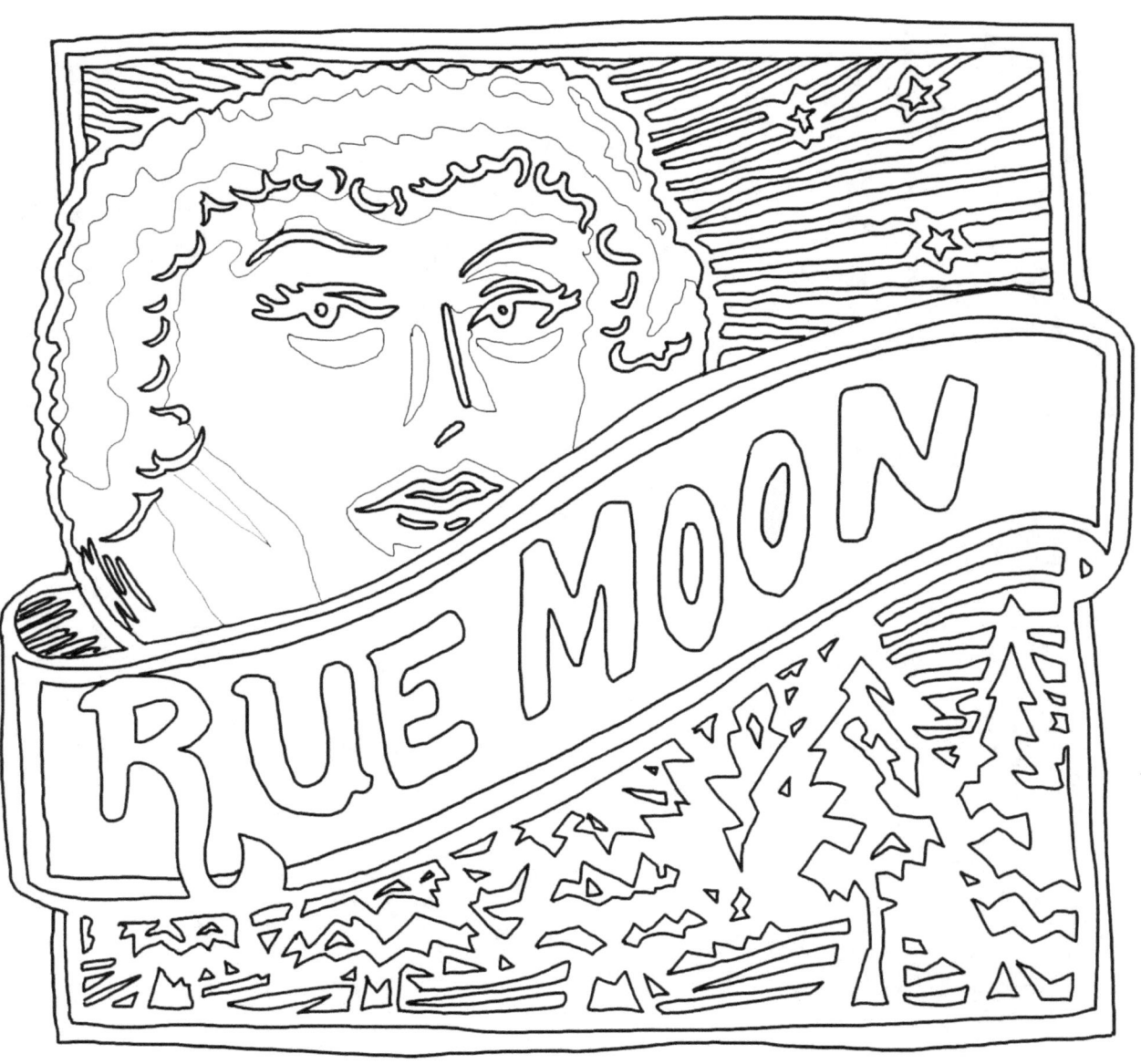

RUE MOON

#RueTheDay 49/365

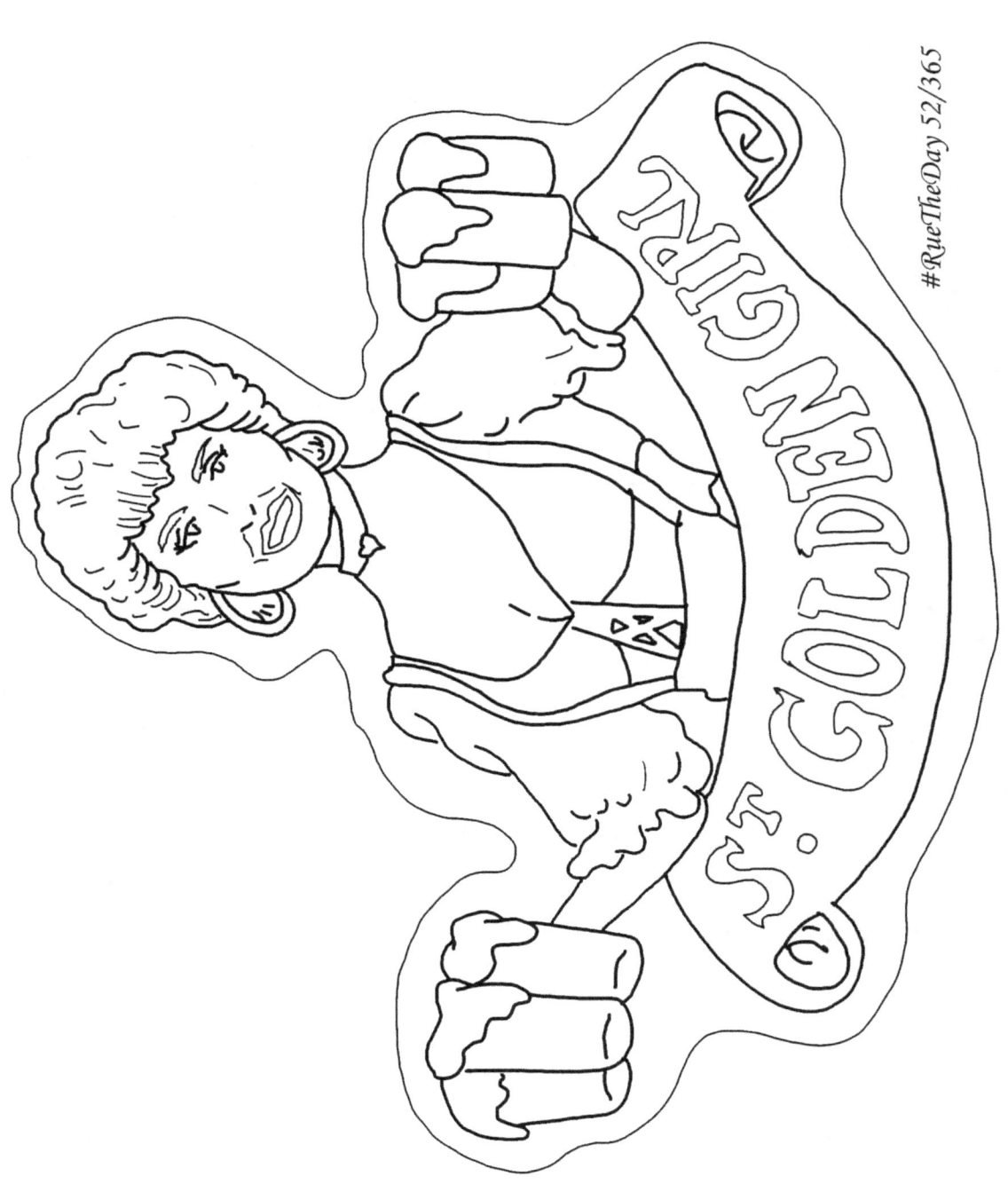

St. GOLDEN GIRL

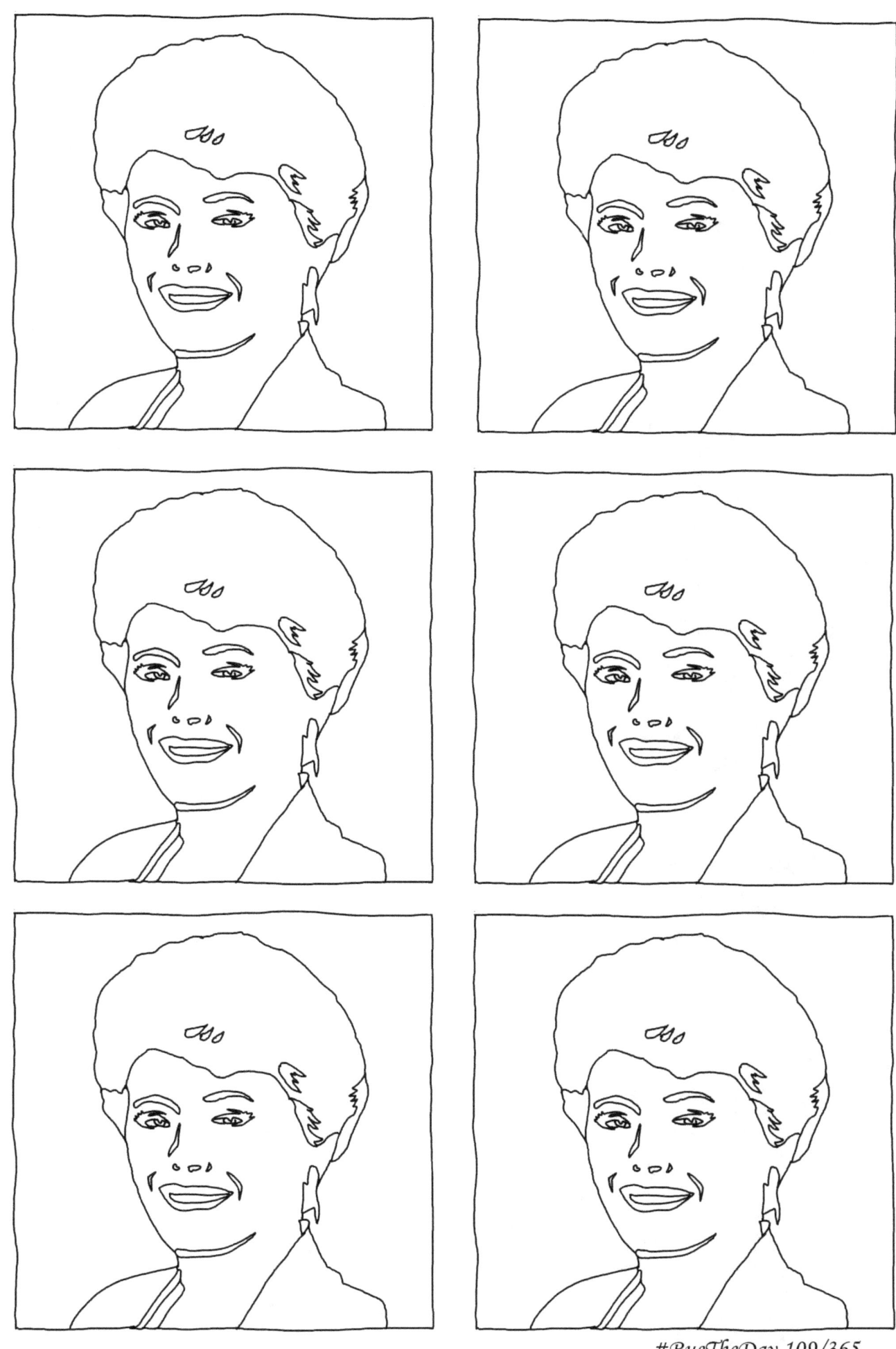

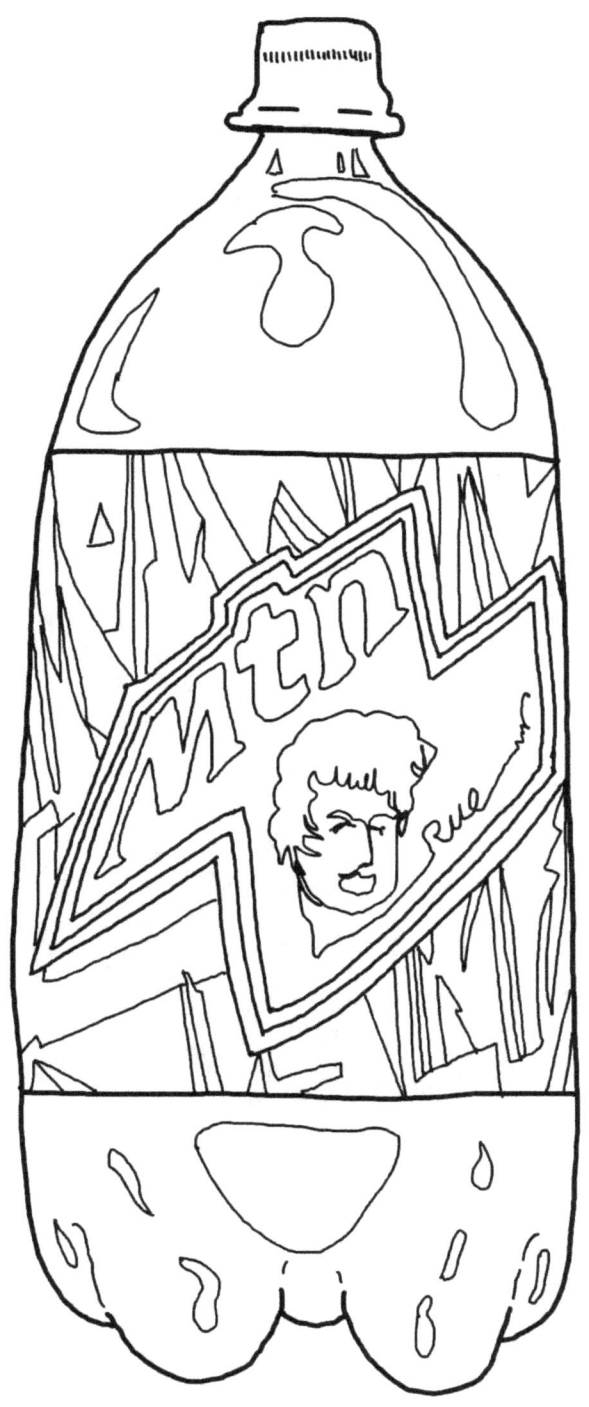

SLUT PUPPiE

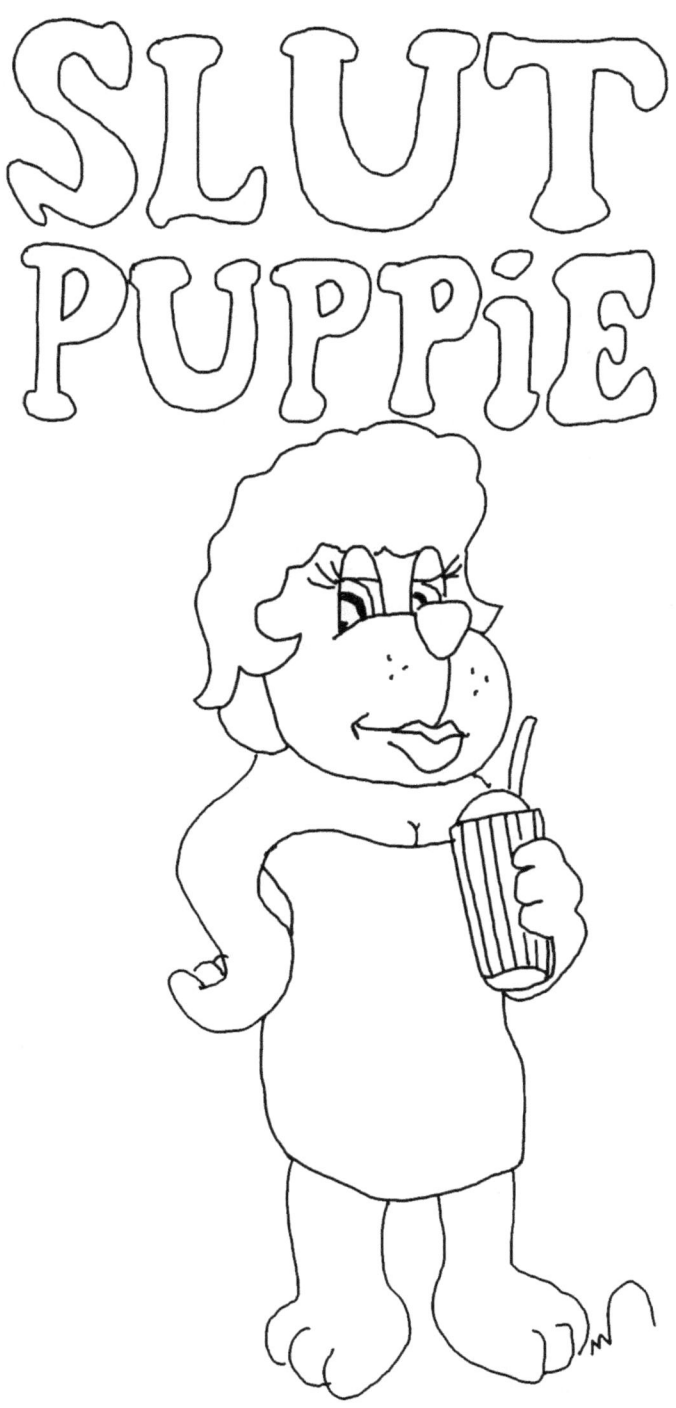

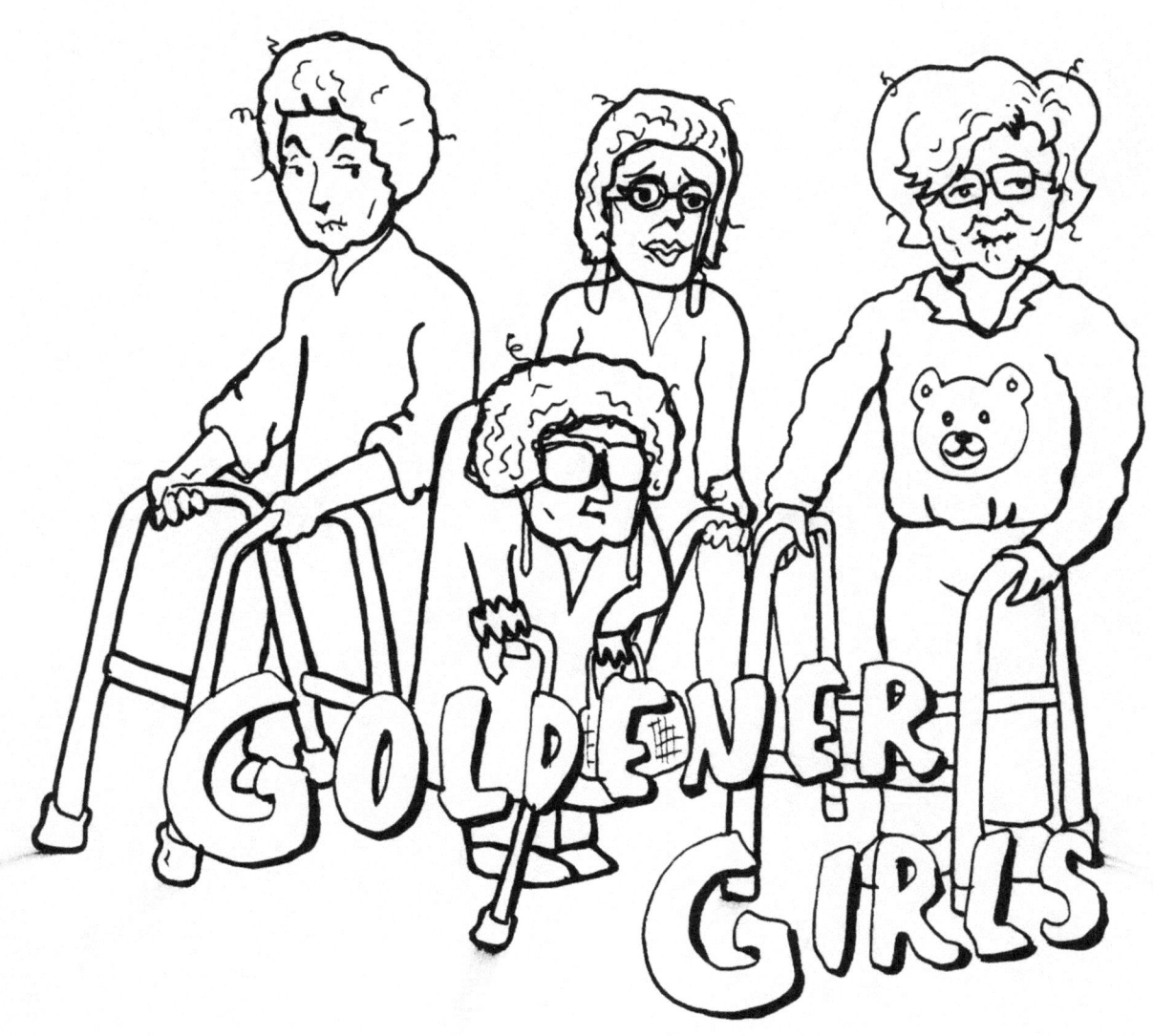

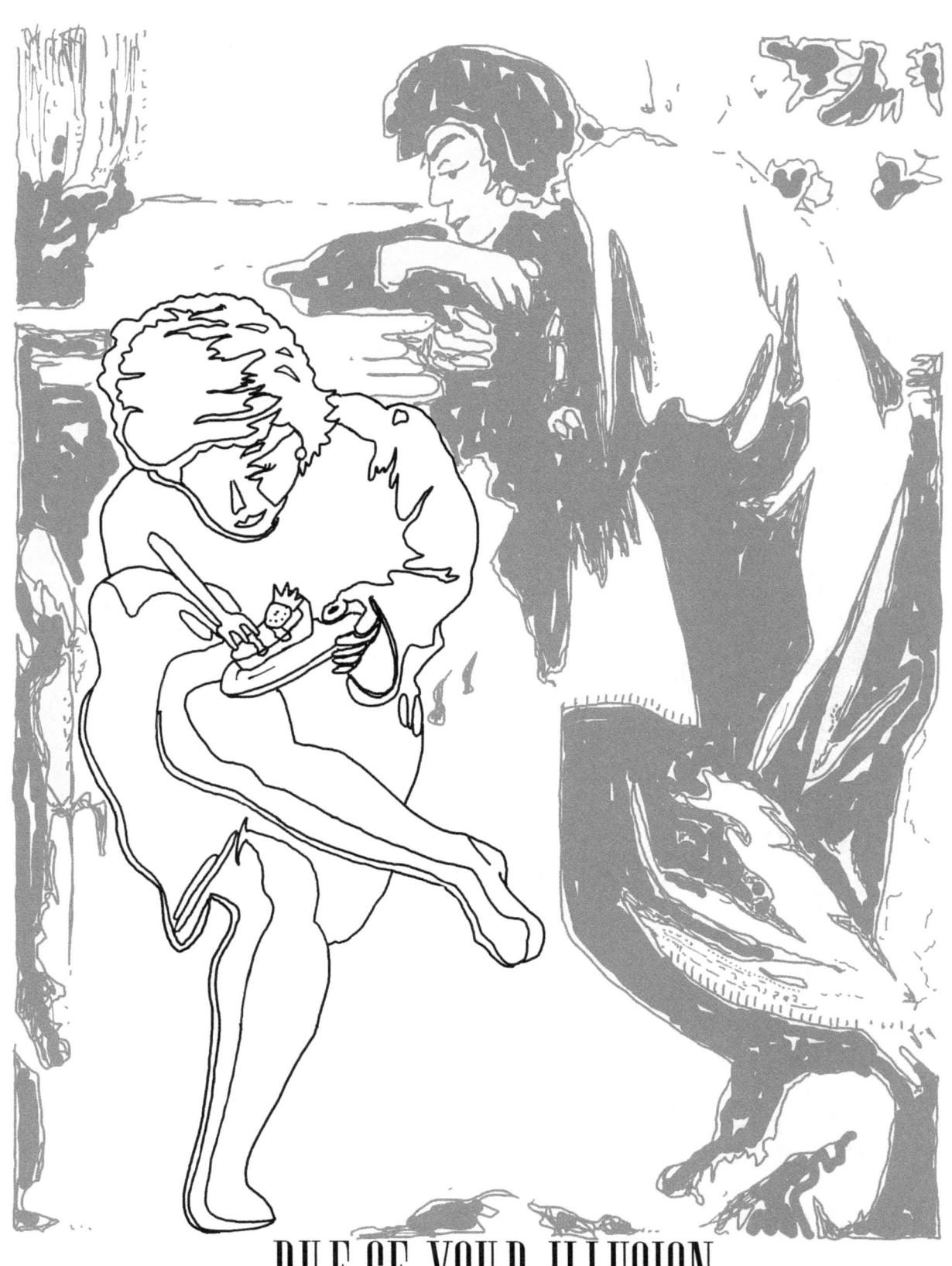

RUE-SE YOUR ILLUSION

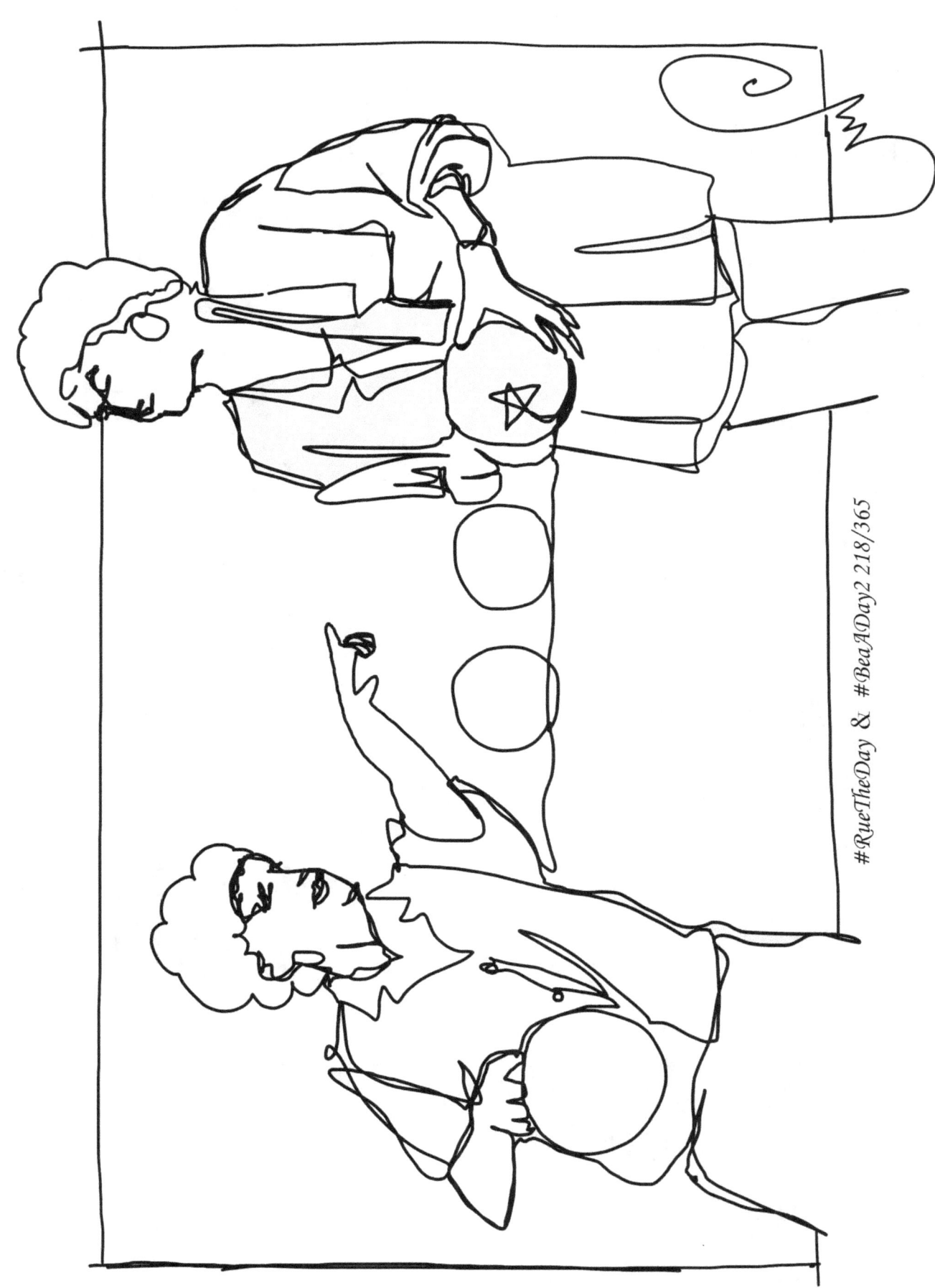

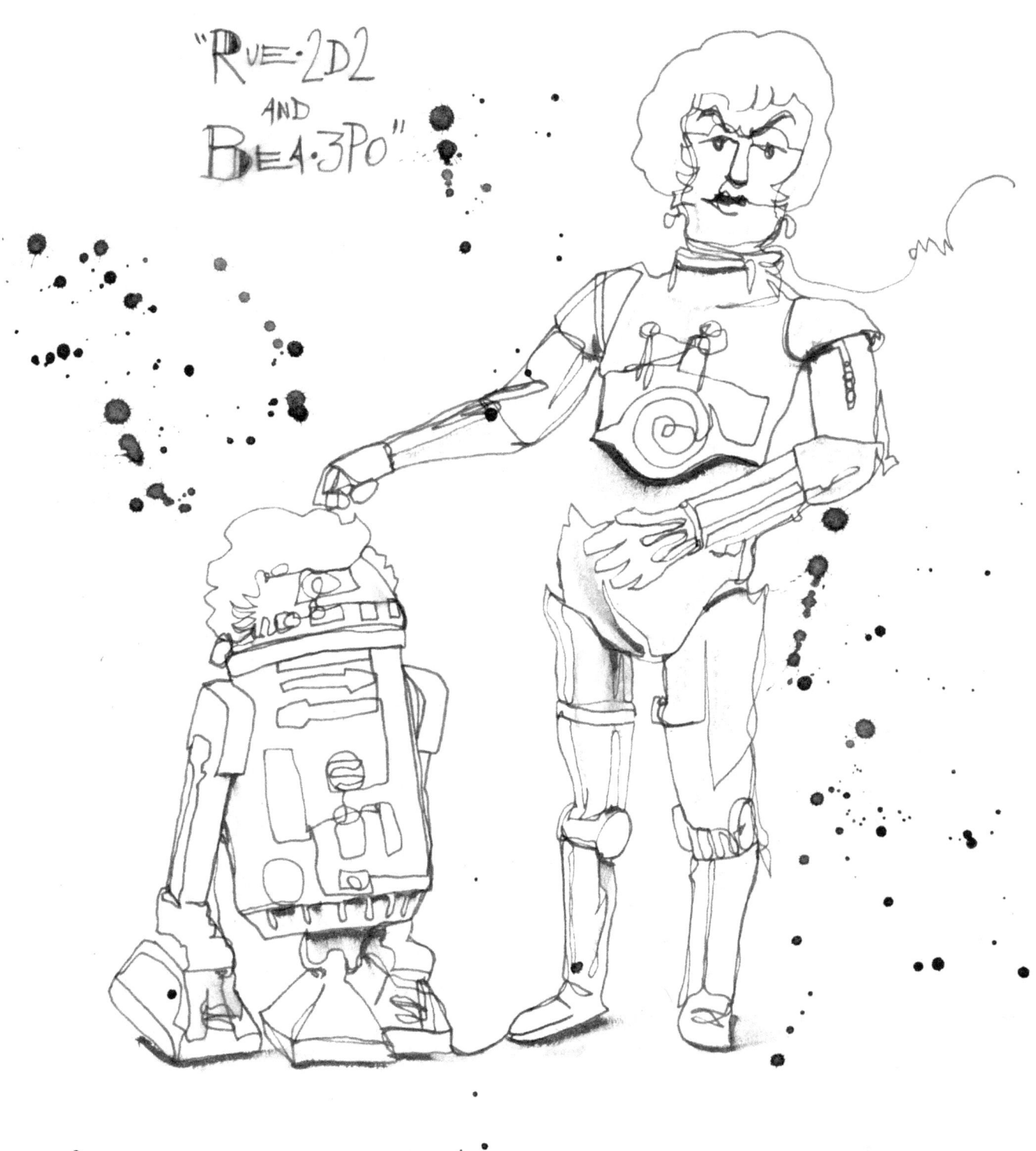

"Rue·2D2 AND Bea·3PO"

4. #BeaADay2

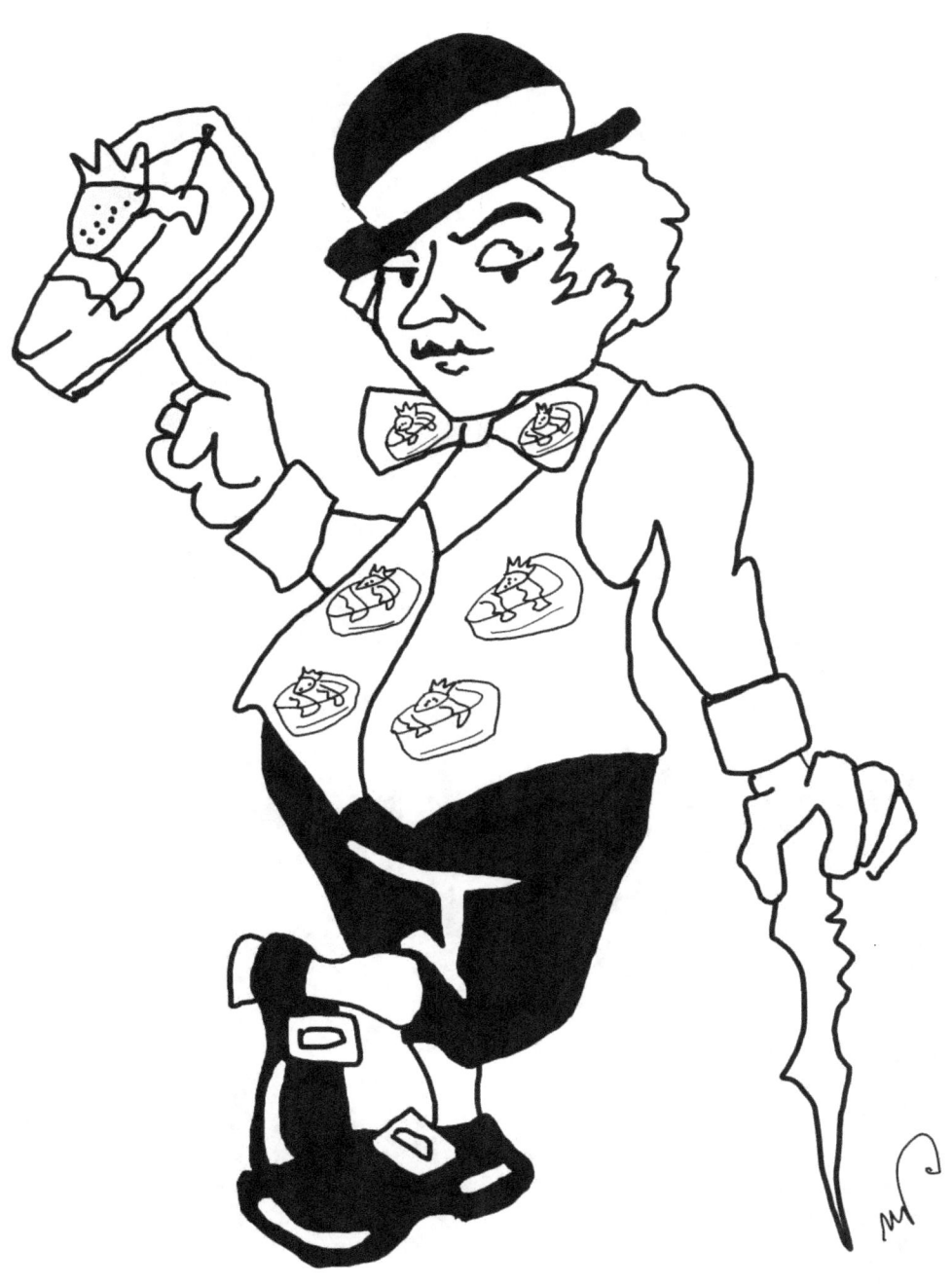

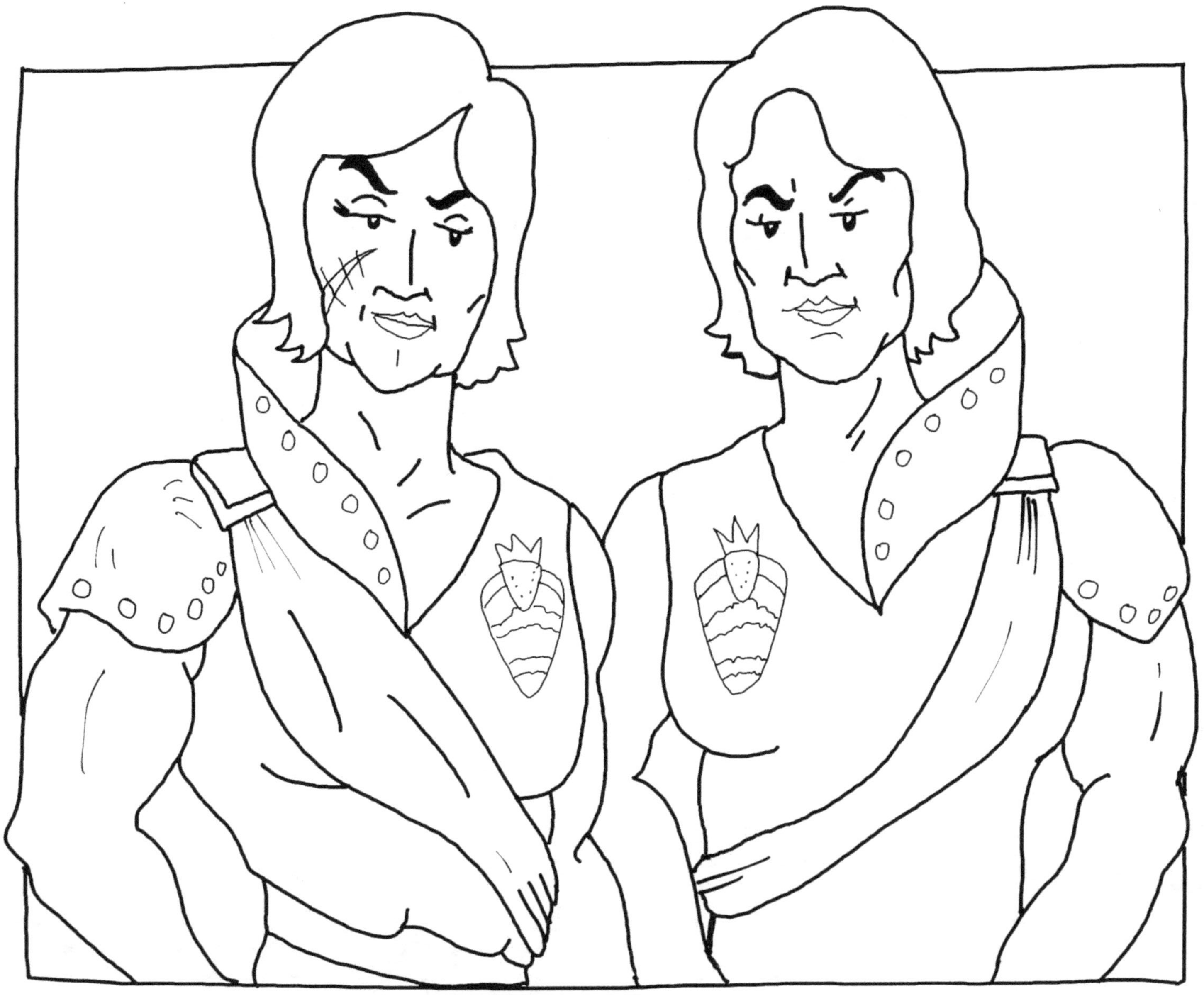

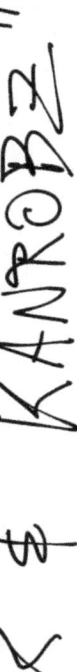

"ZBORNAK & KANROBZ"

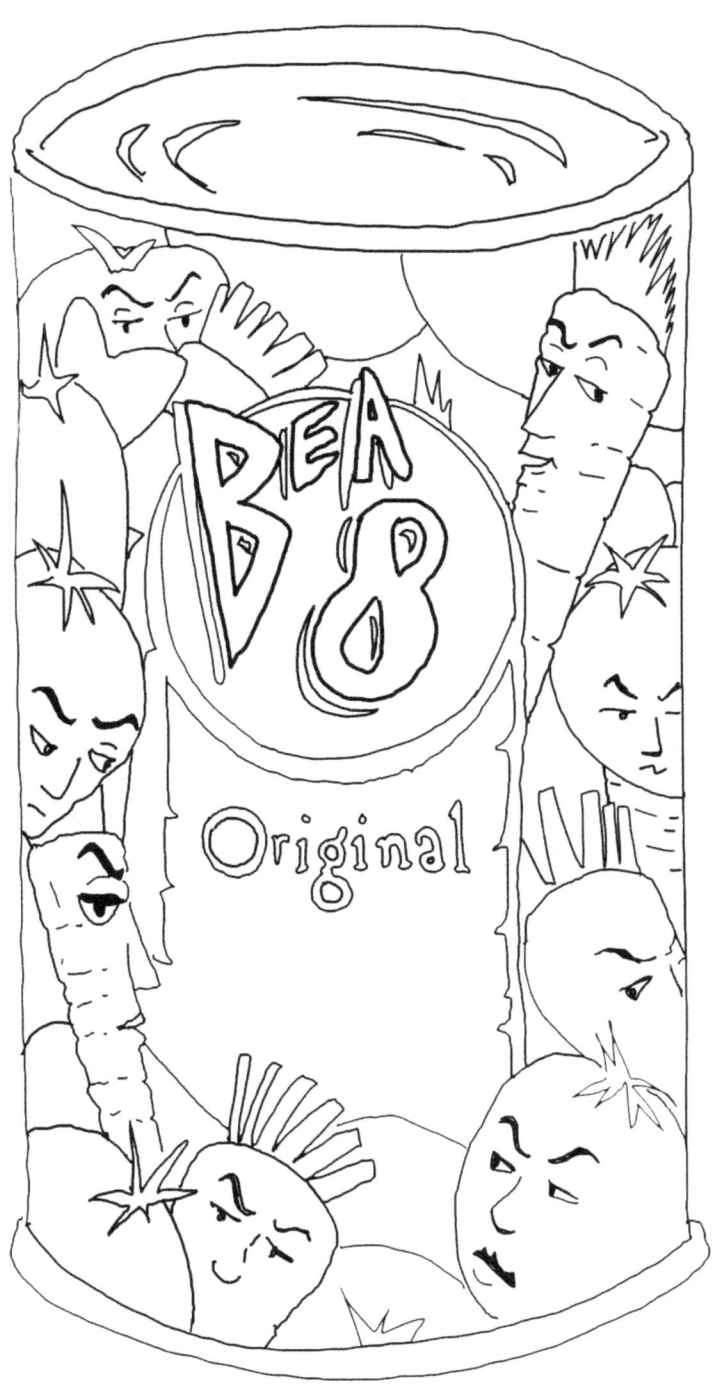

BeA 8

Original

#BeaADay 142/365

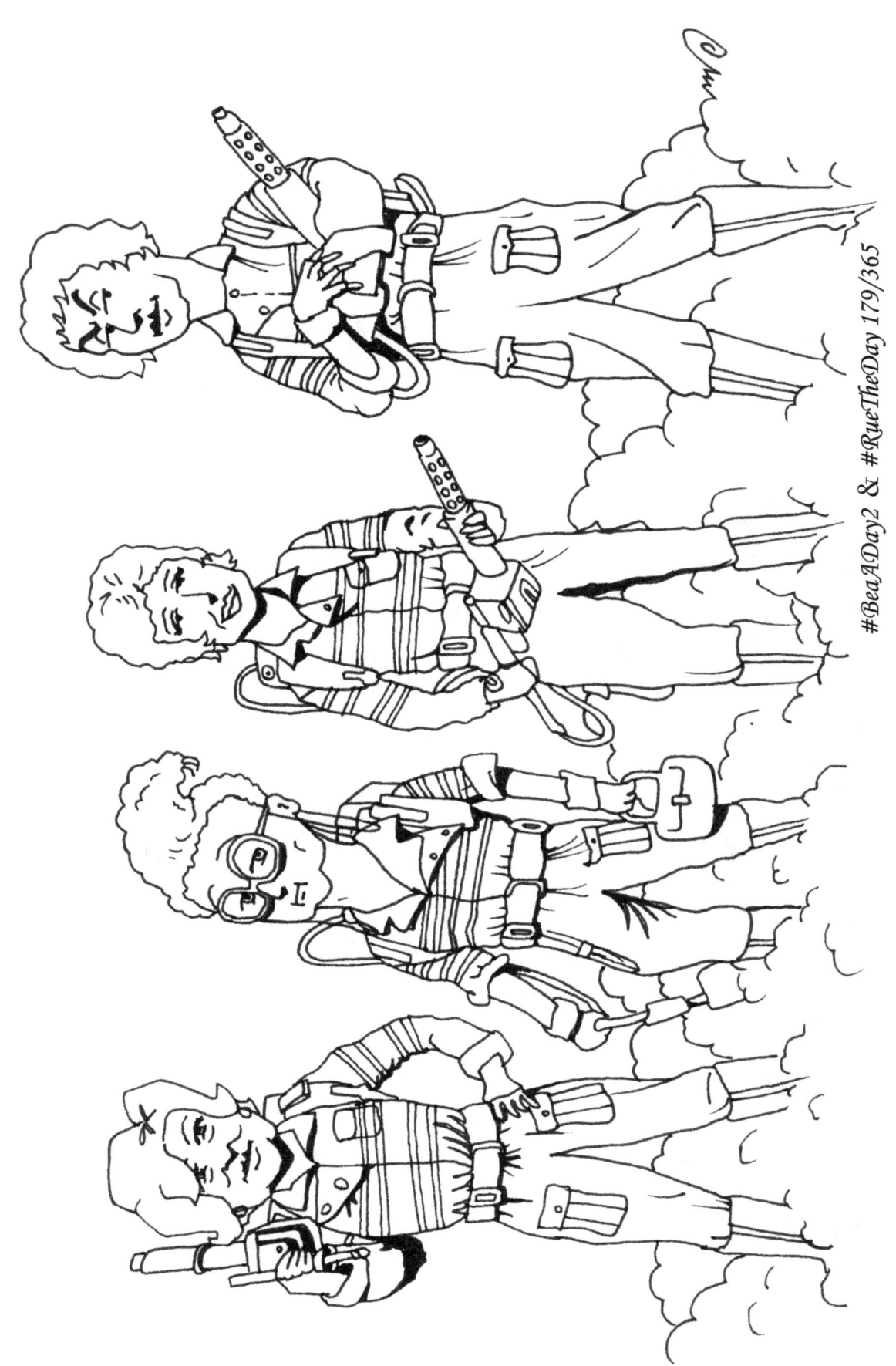

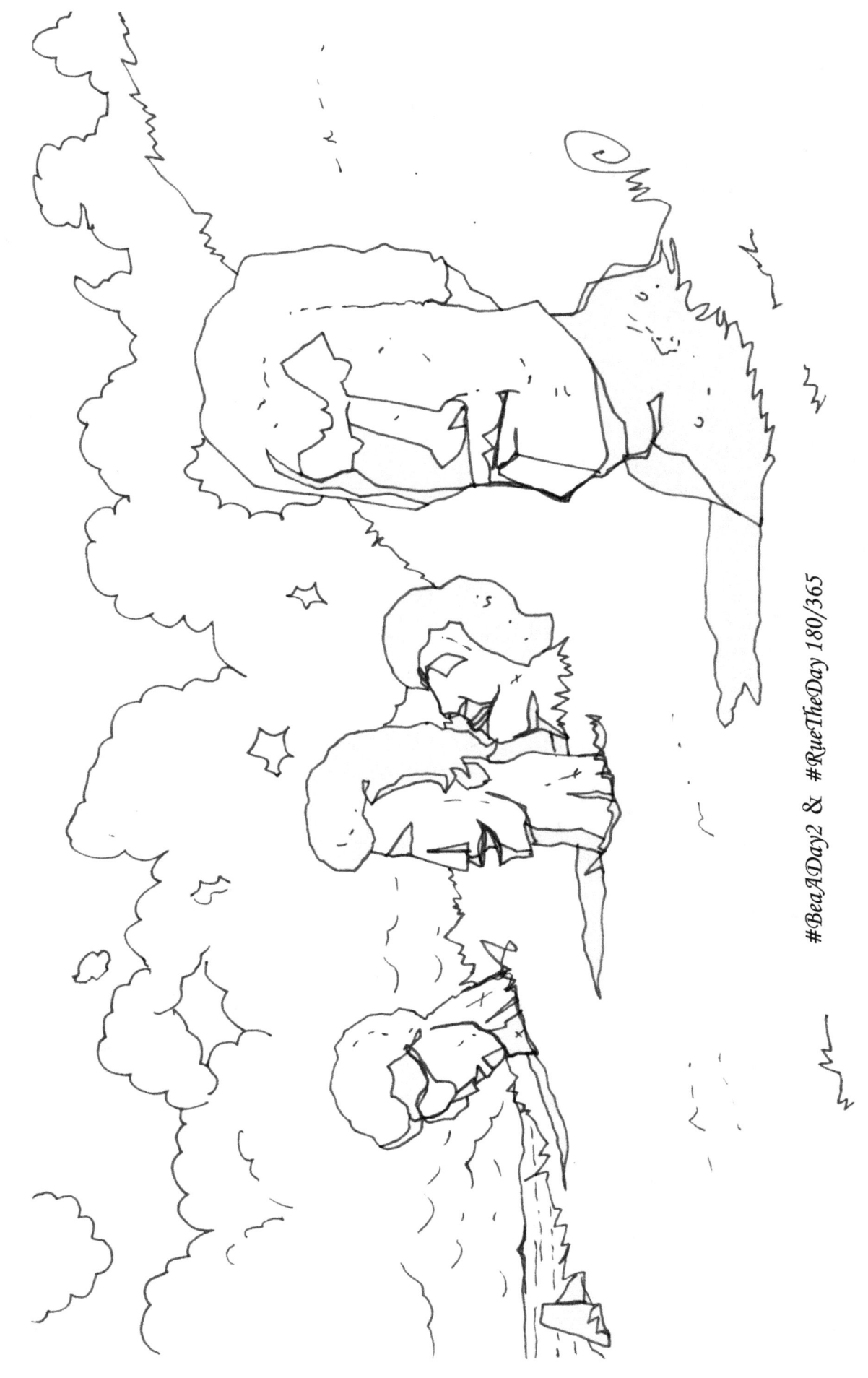

#BeaADay2 & #RueTheDay 180/365

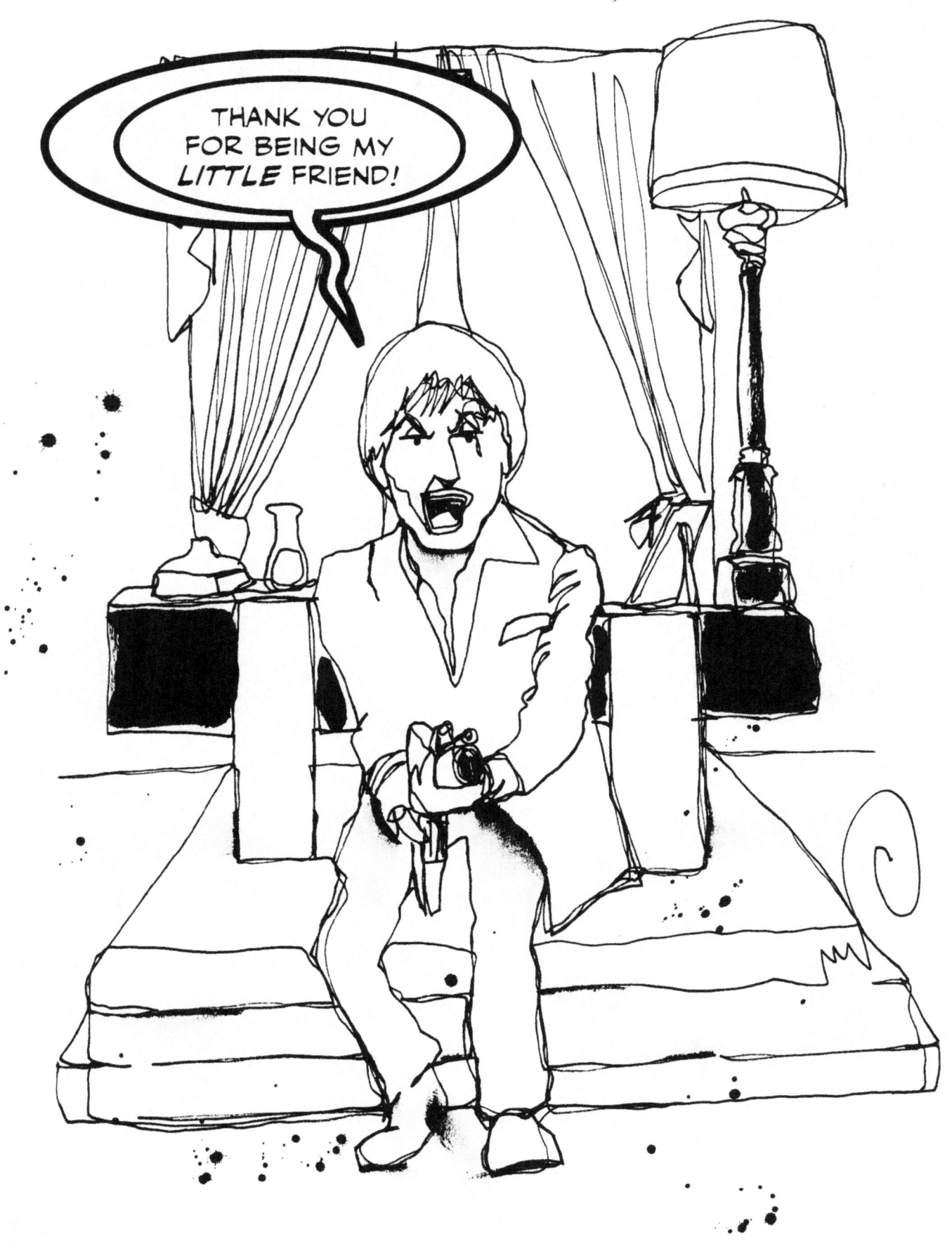

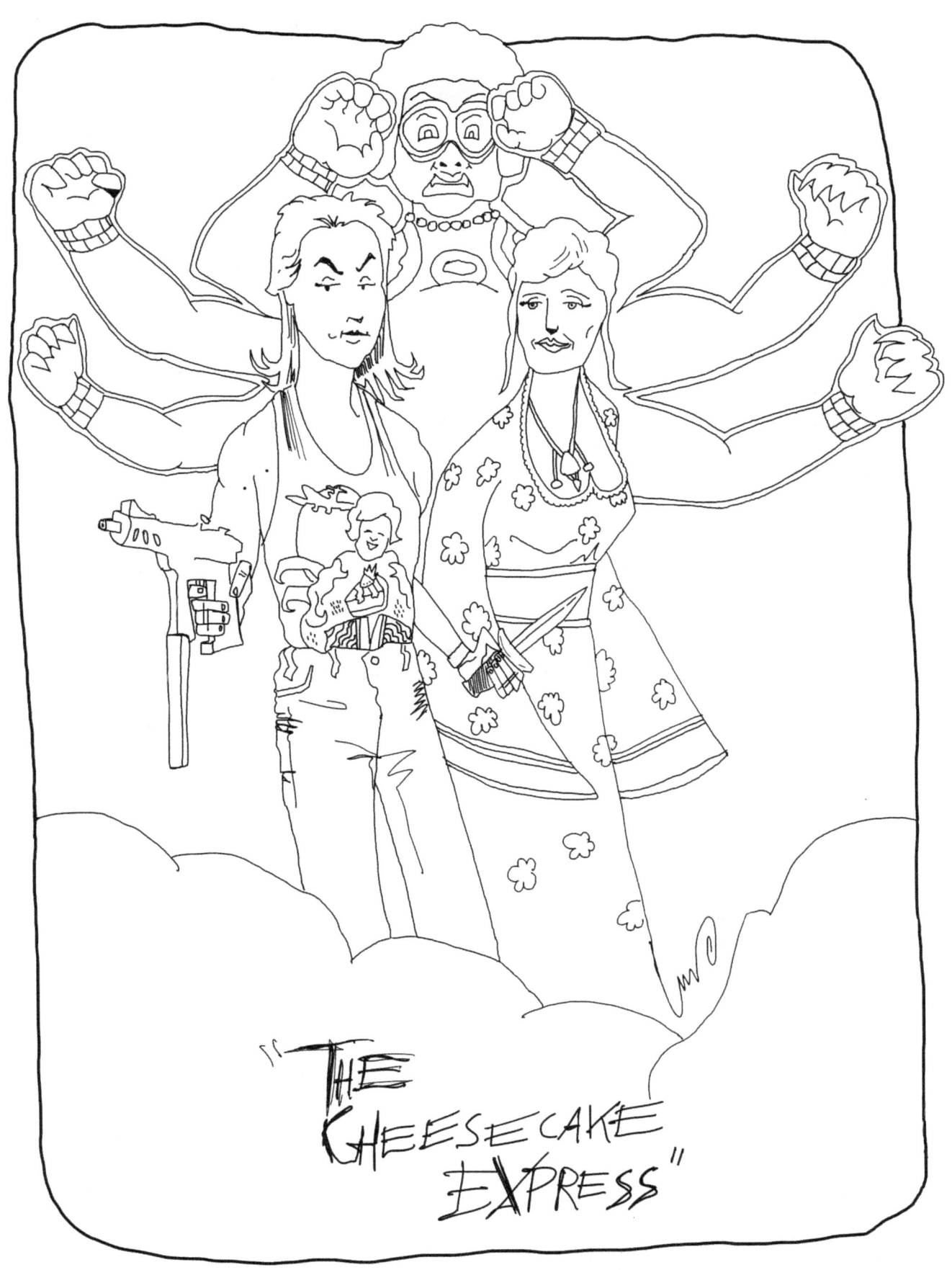

"THE CHEESECAKE EXPRESS"

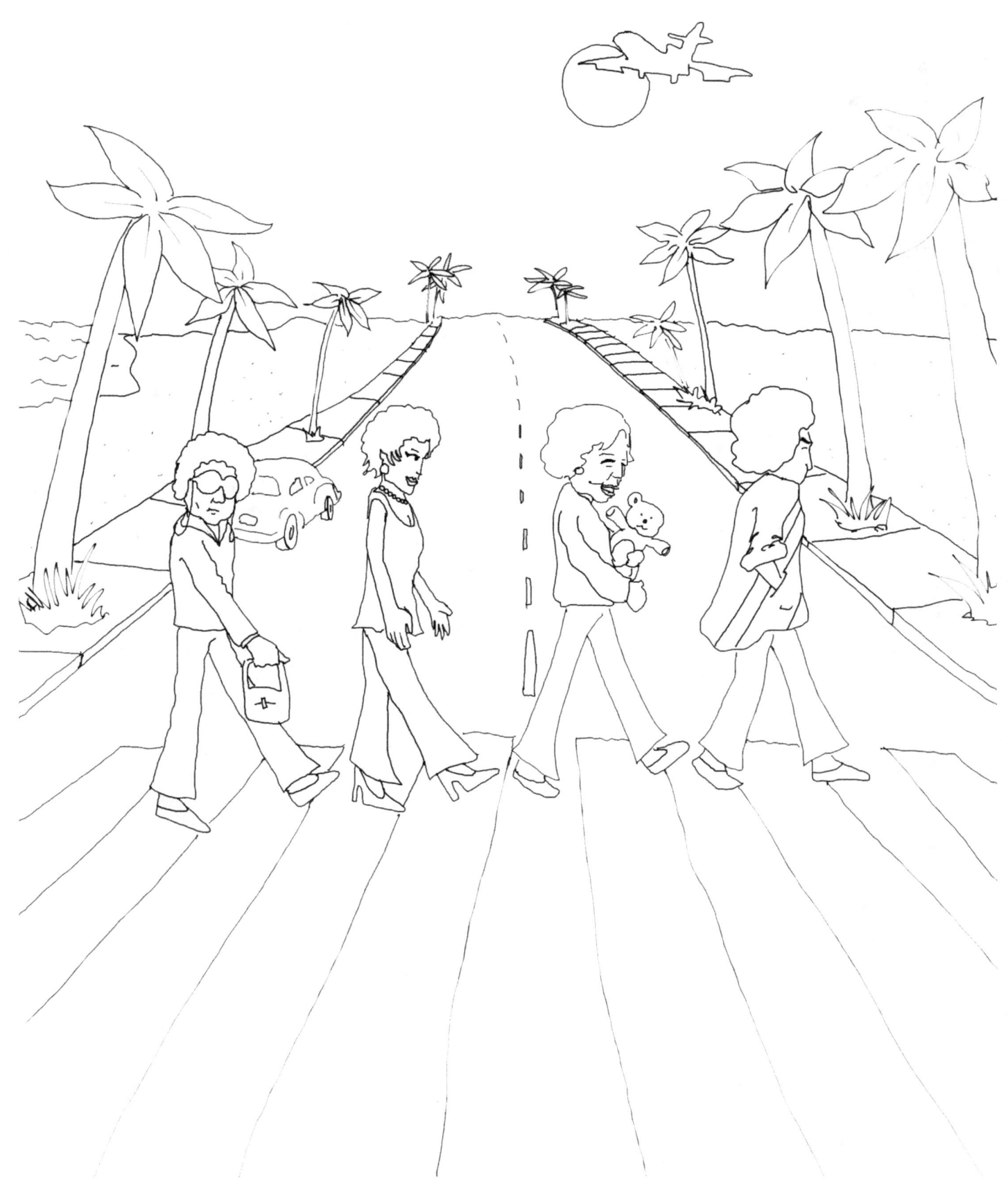

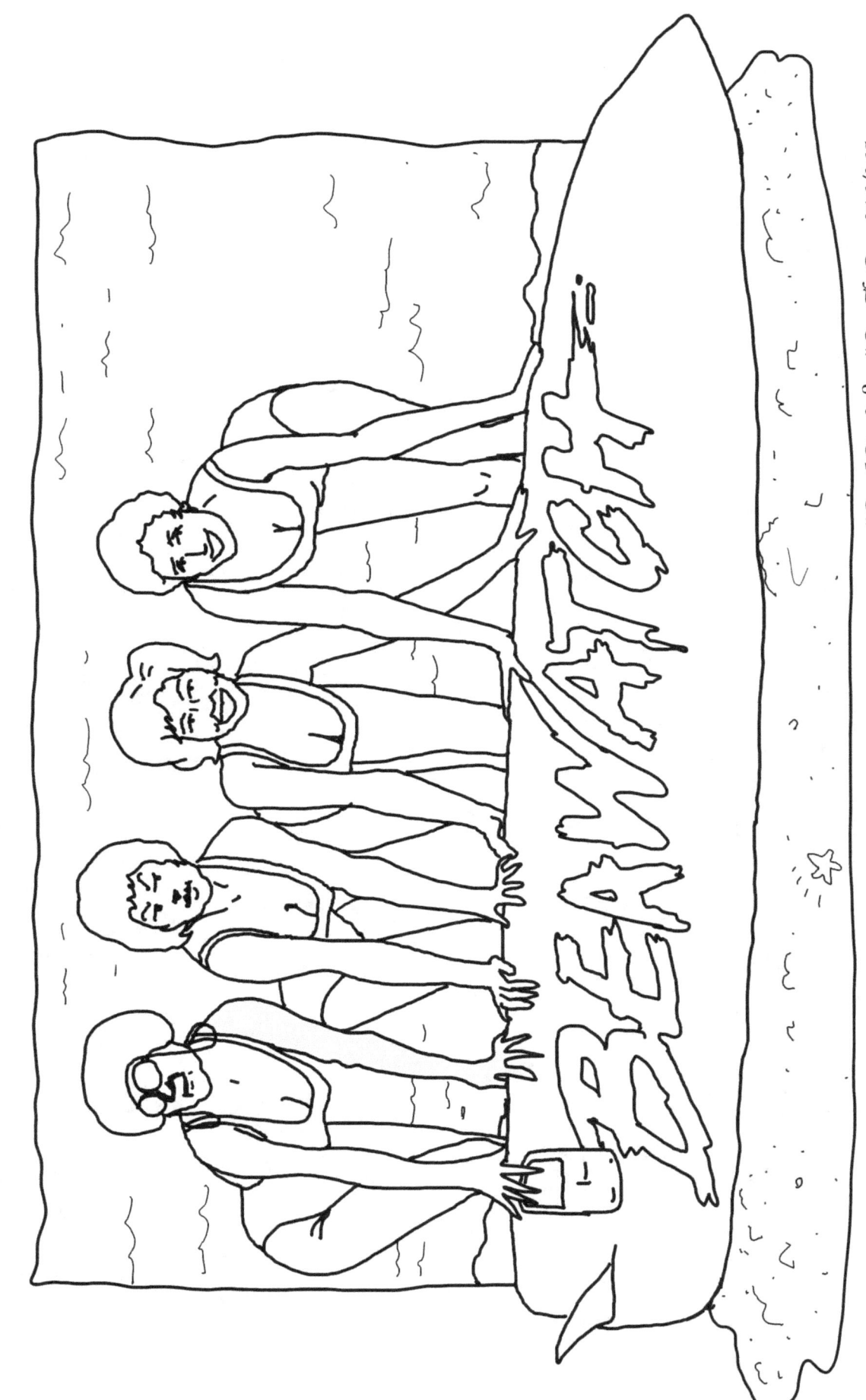

5. BONUS PAGES

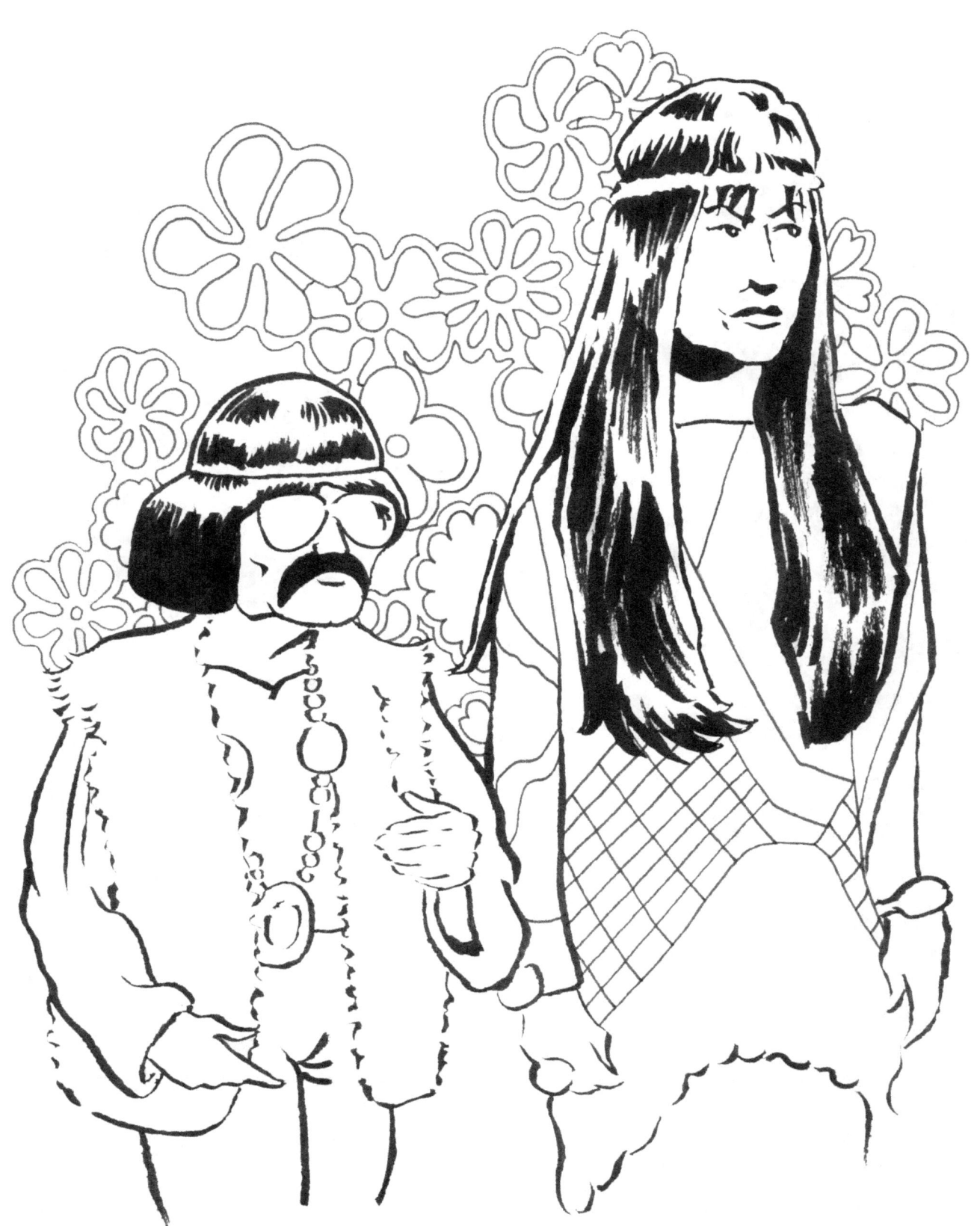

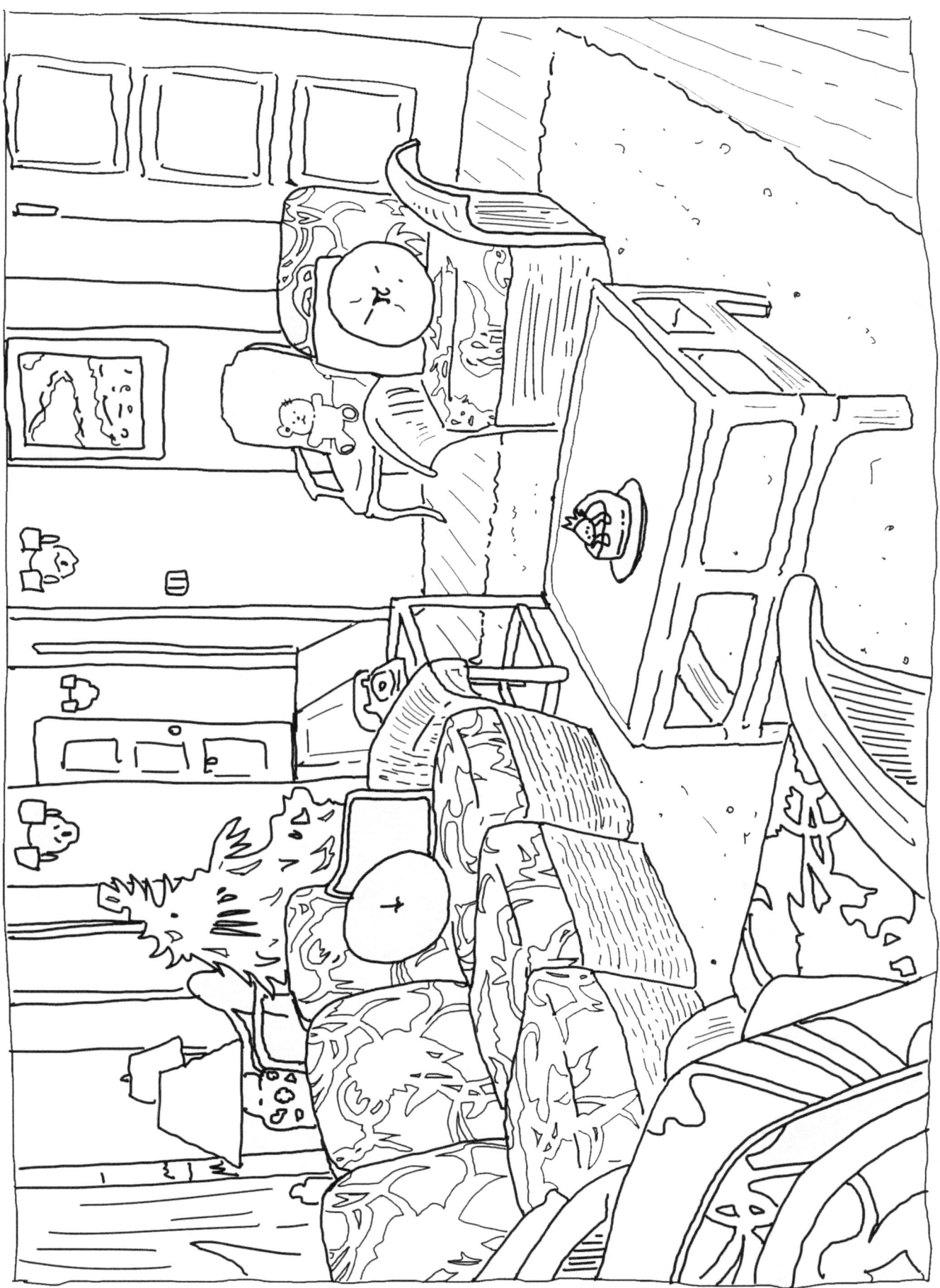

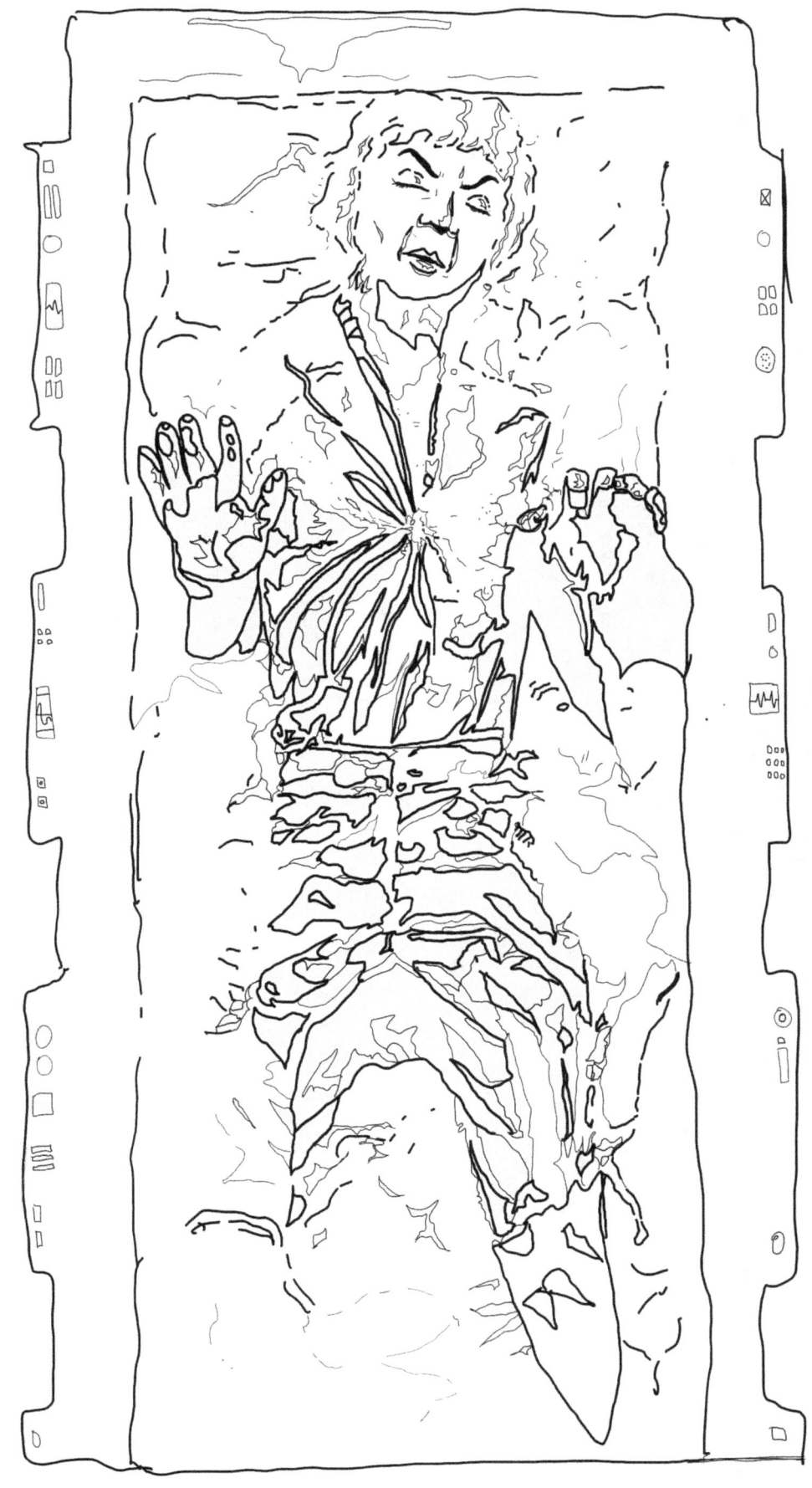

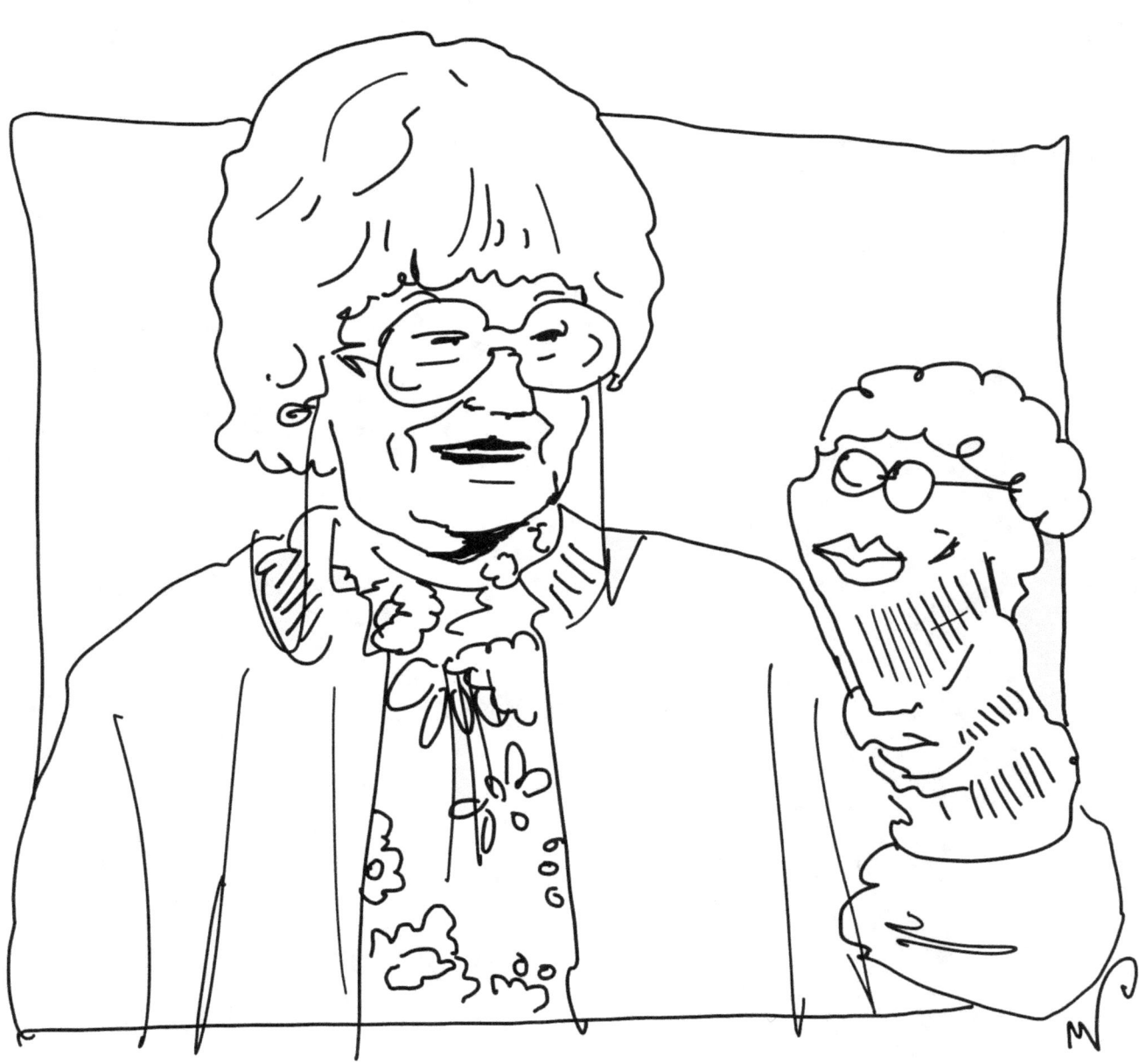

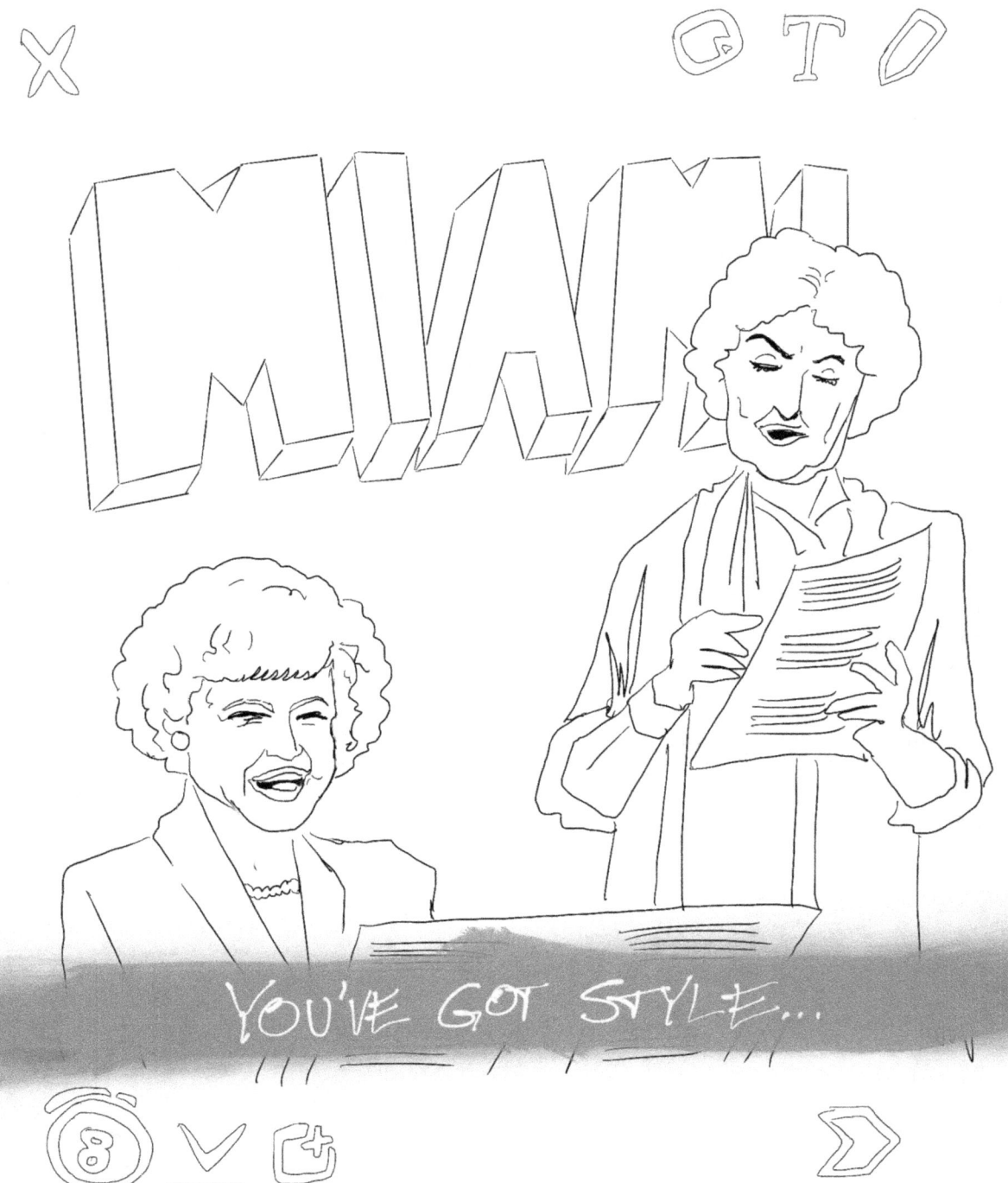

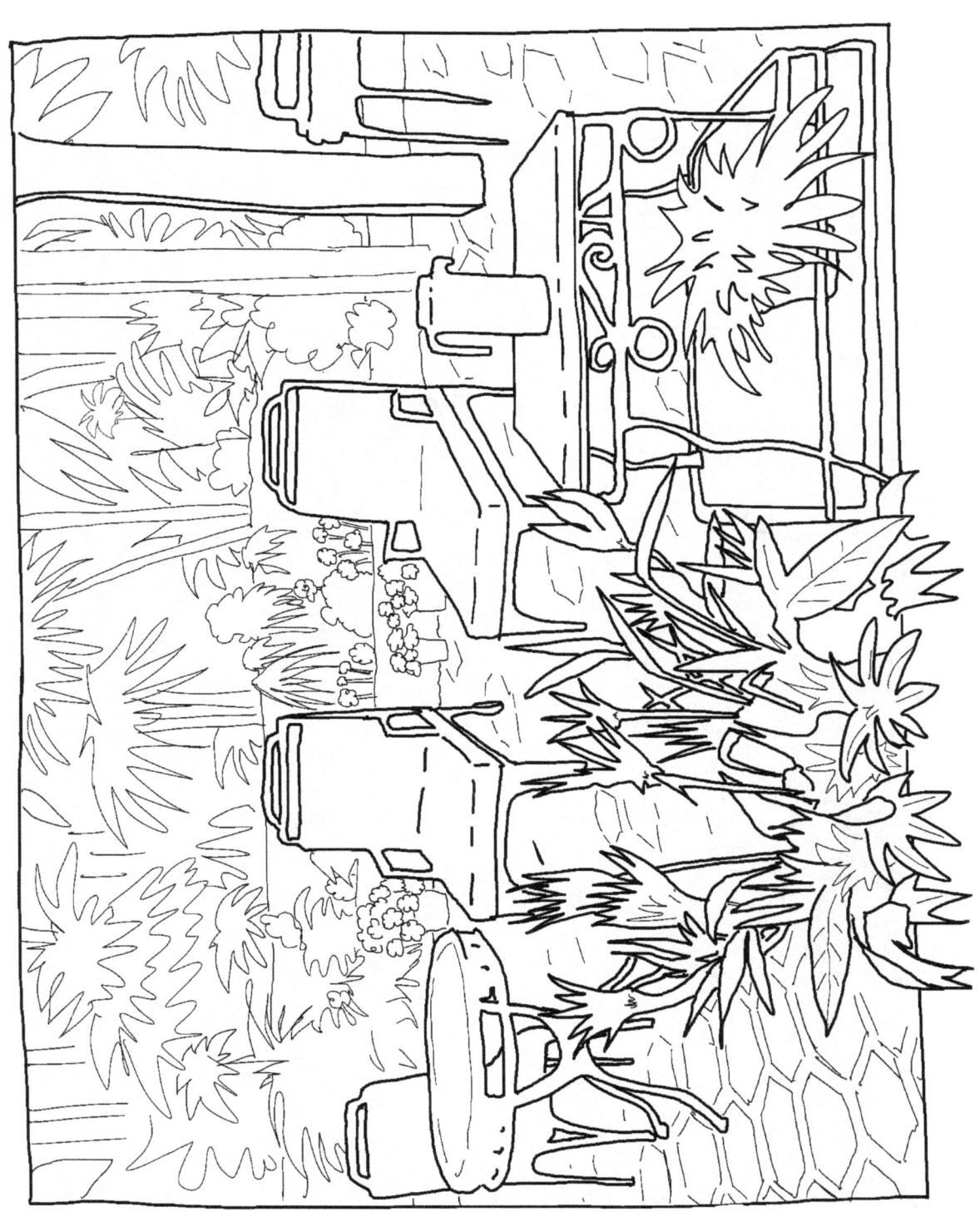

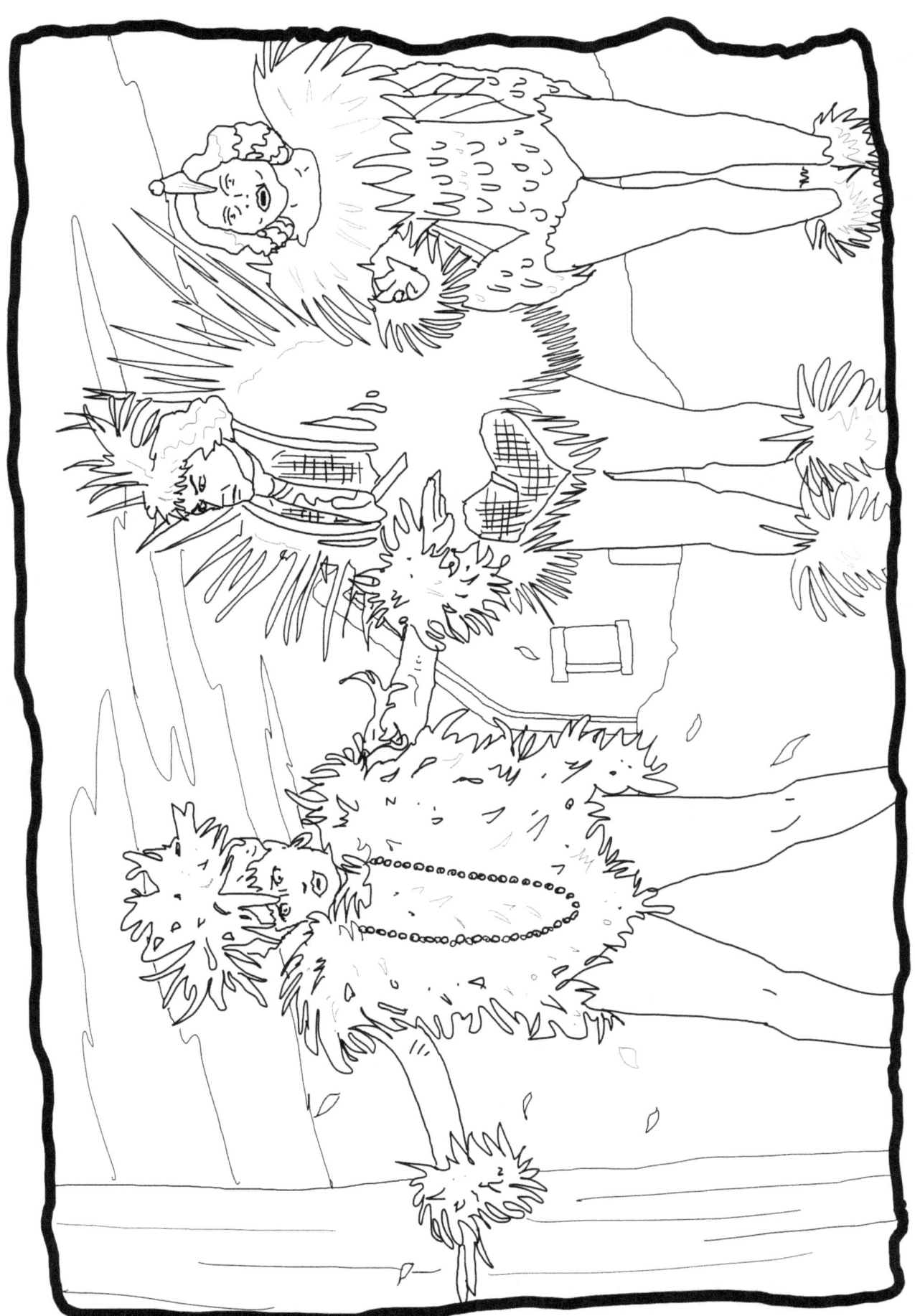

"DoBBEA"

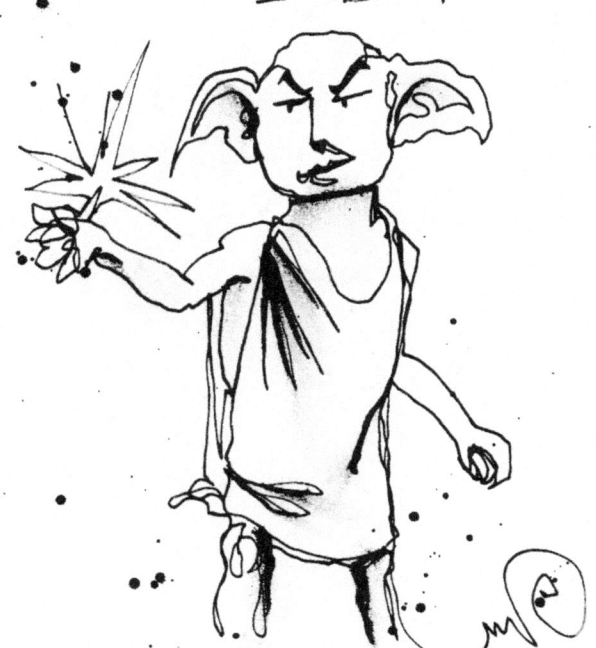

BEAVERUS SNAPE

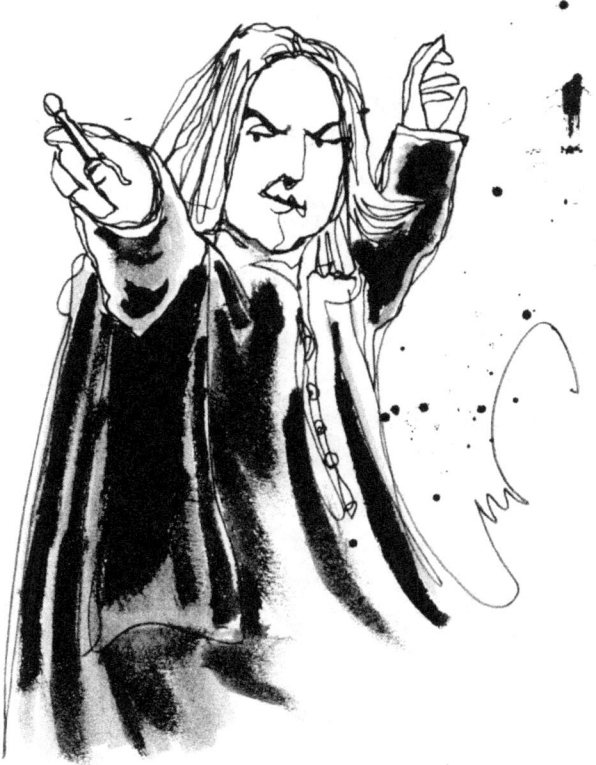

"RUE·BUS HAGRID"

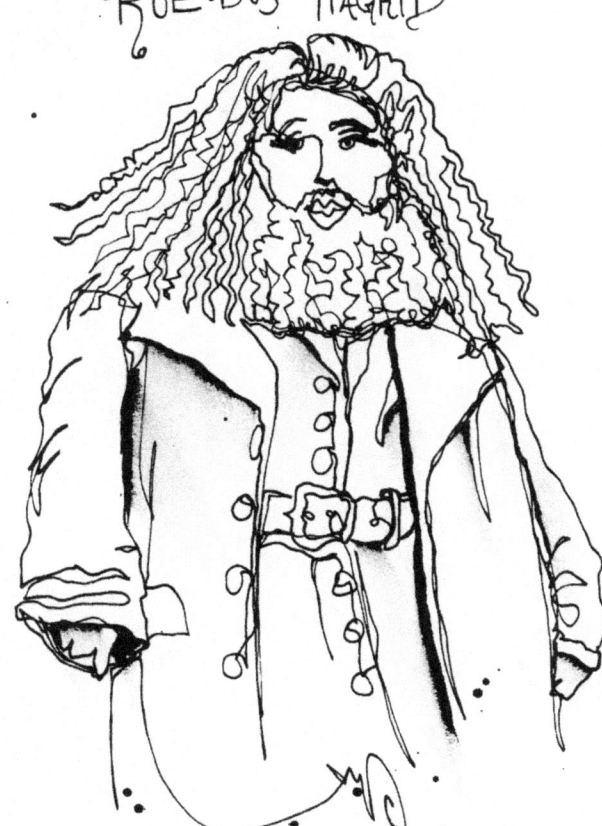

"HARRBEA POTTER"

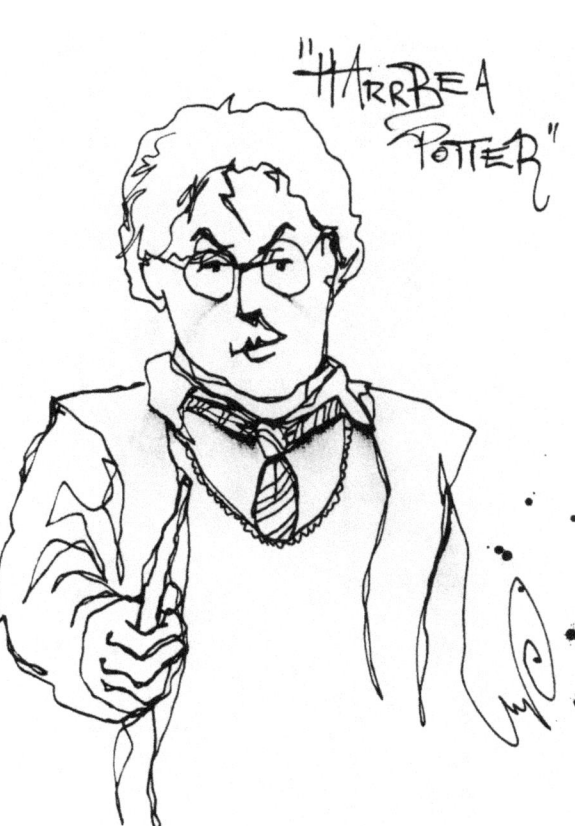

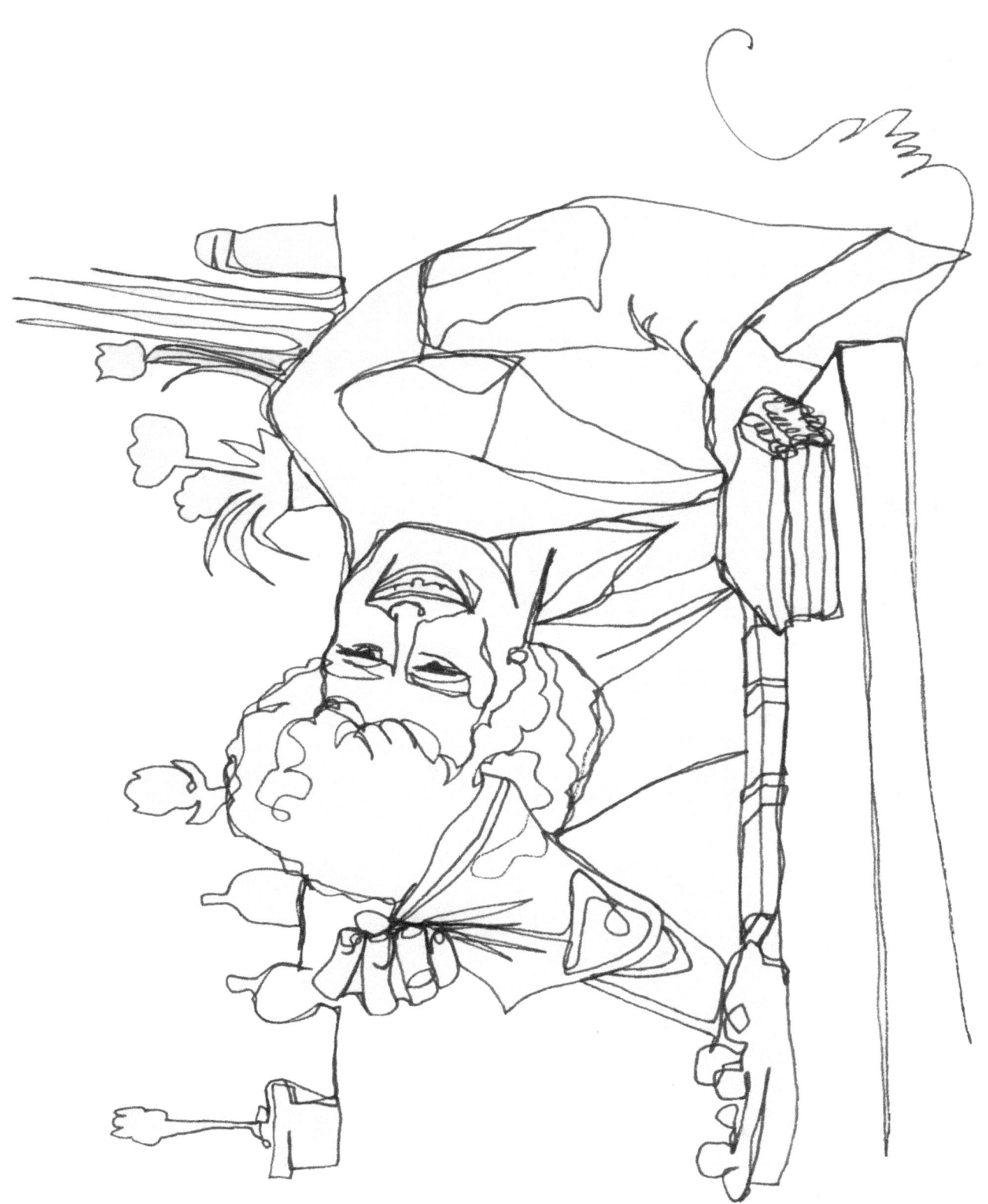

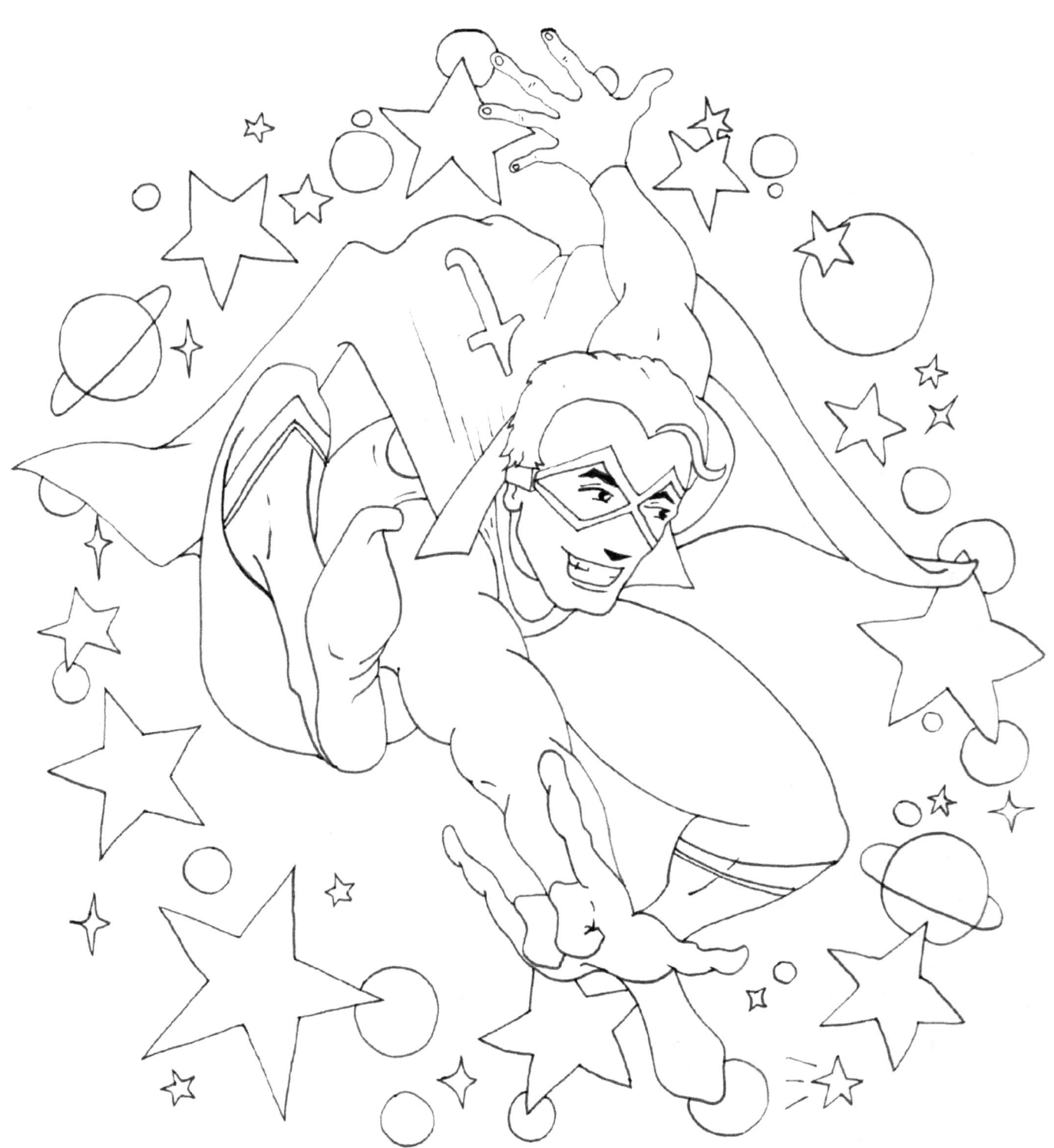

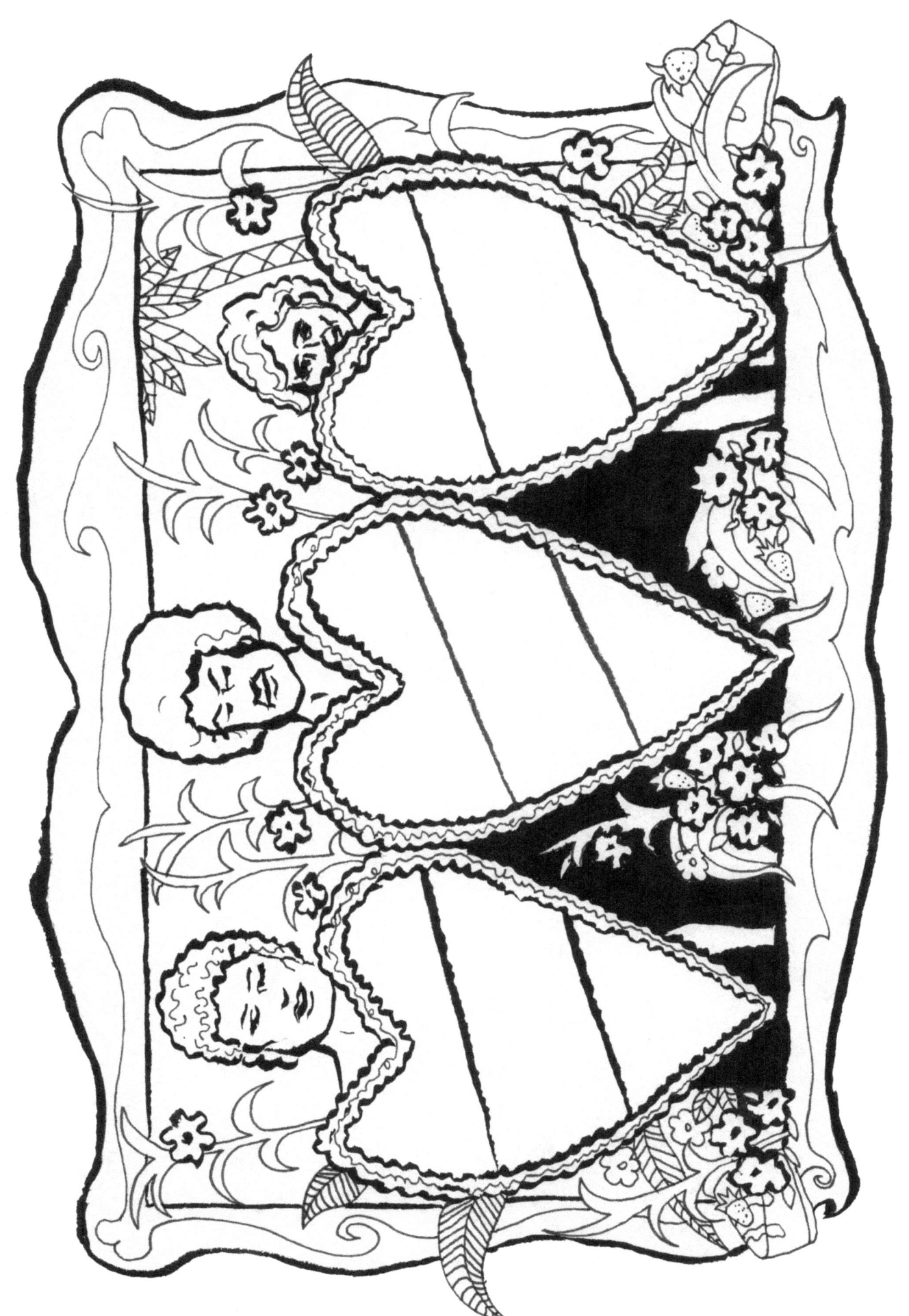

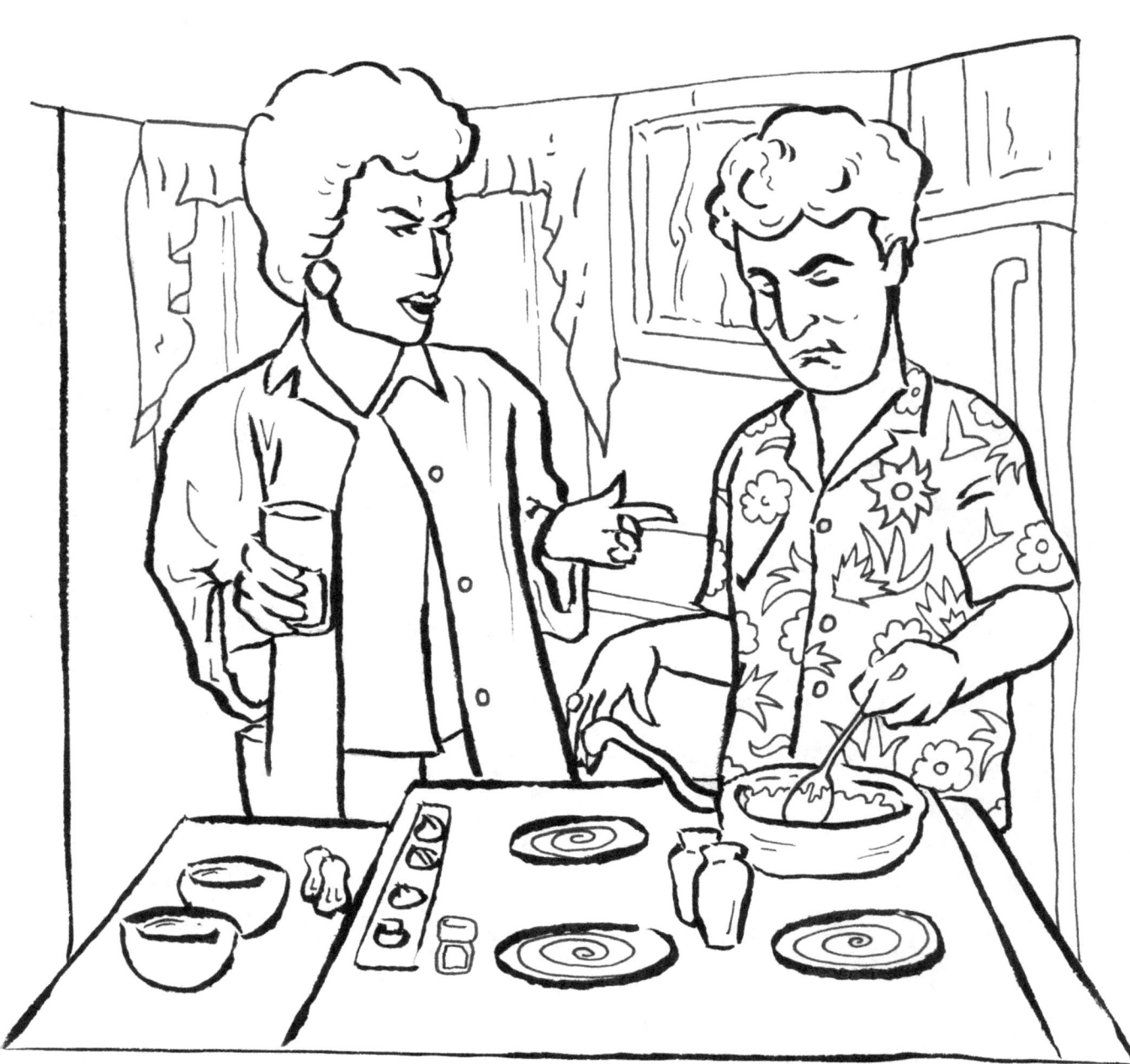

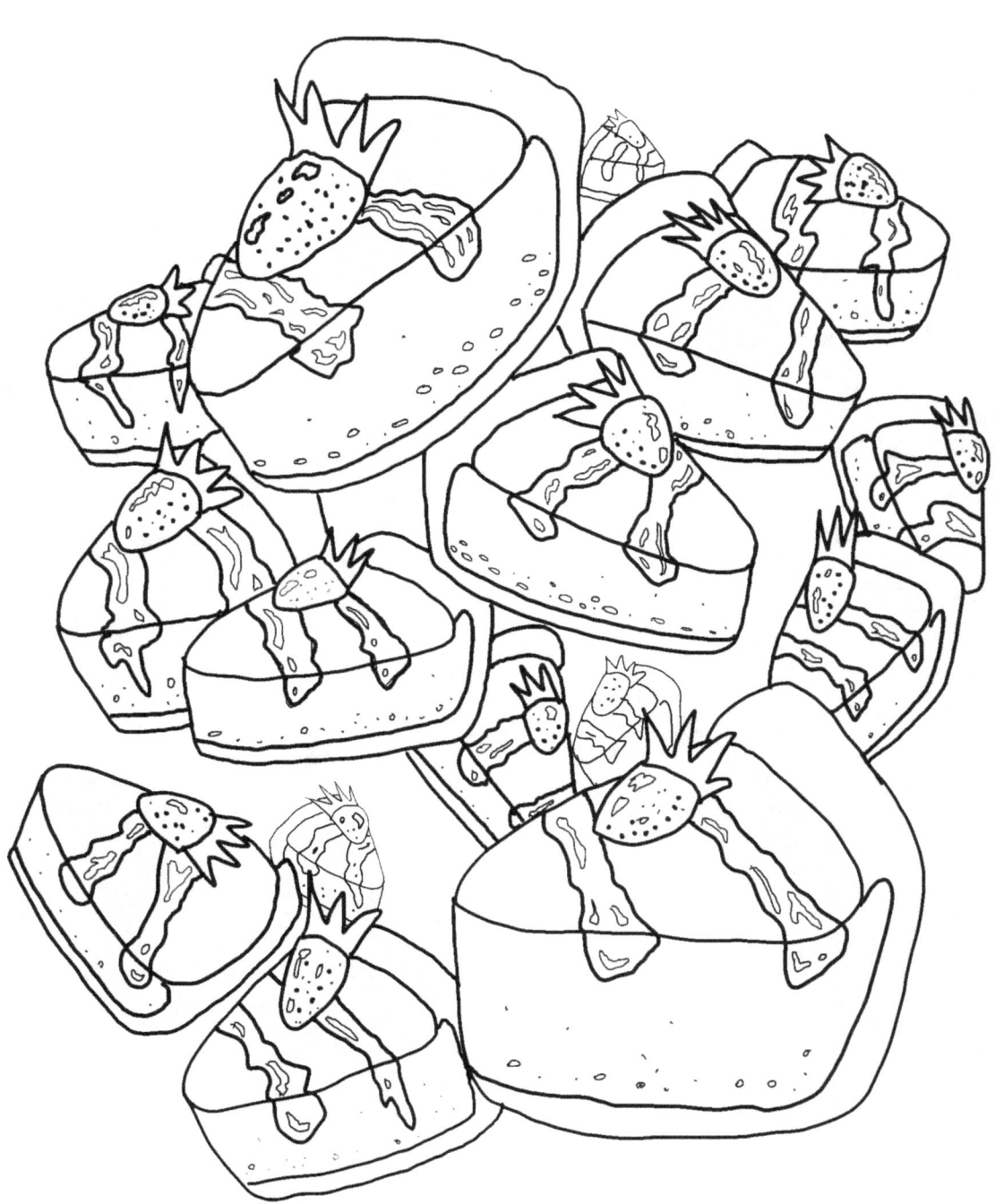

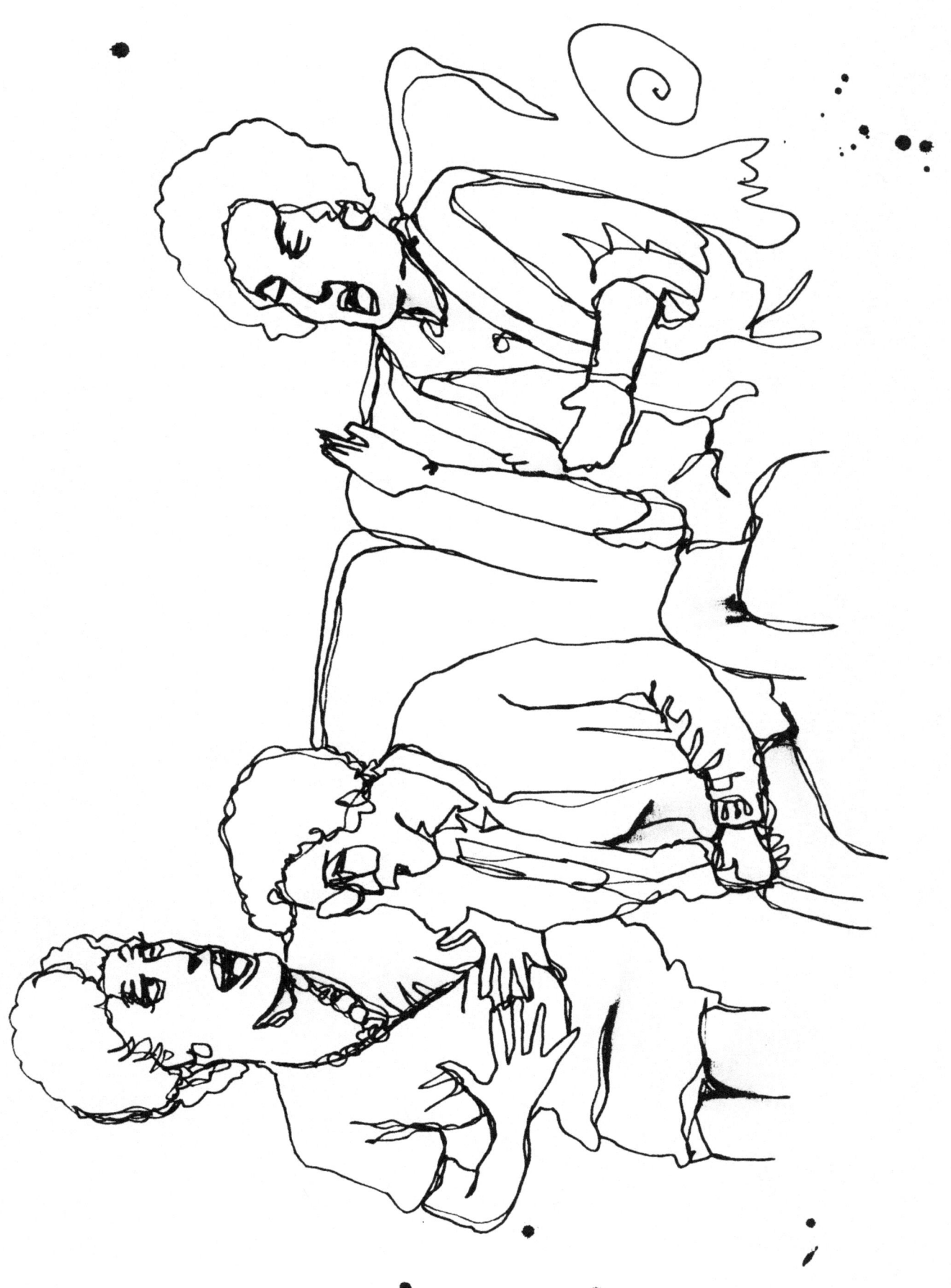

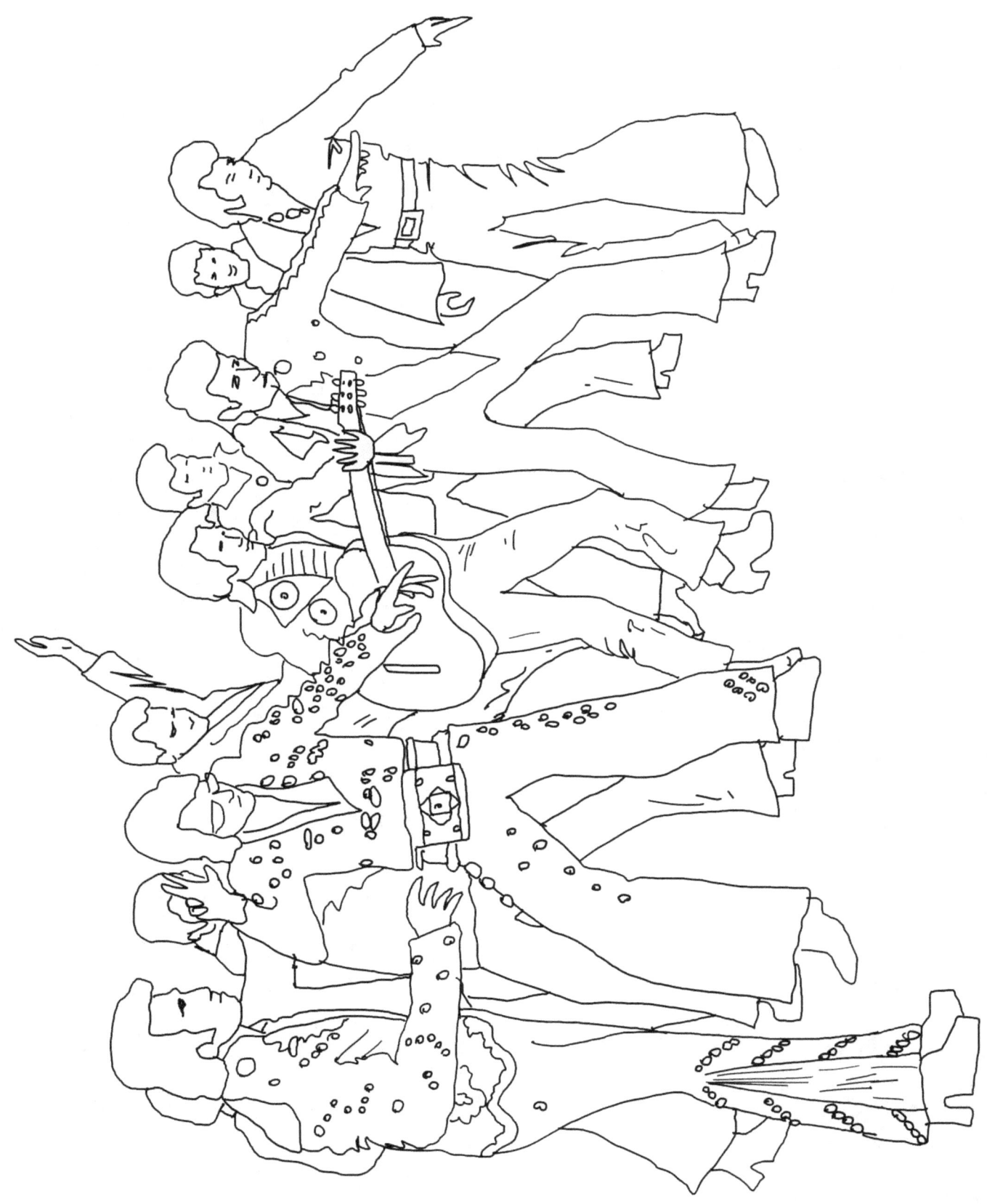

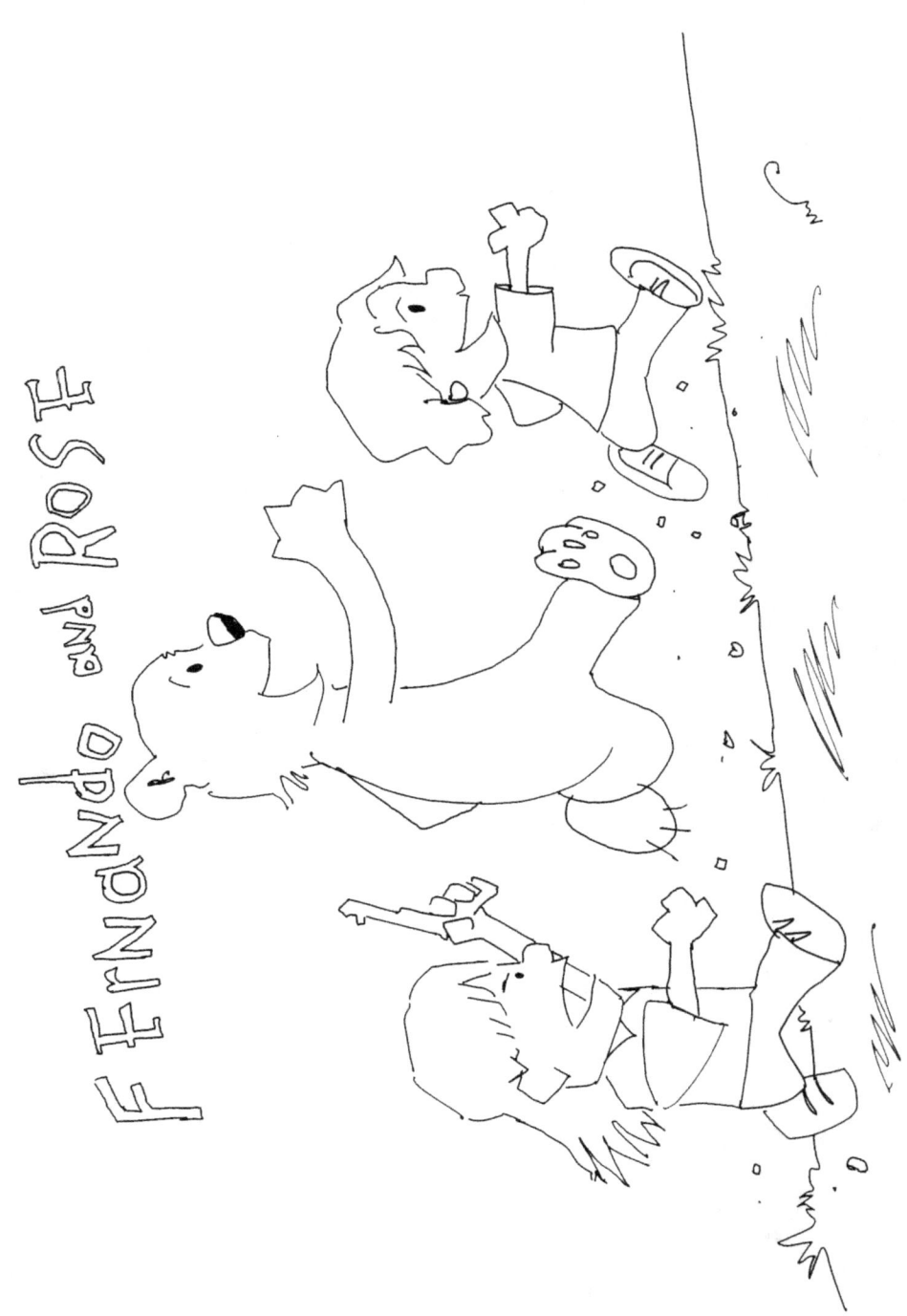

Ffrnando and Rose

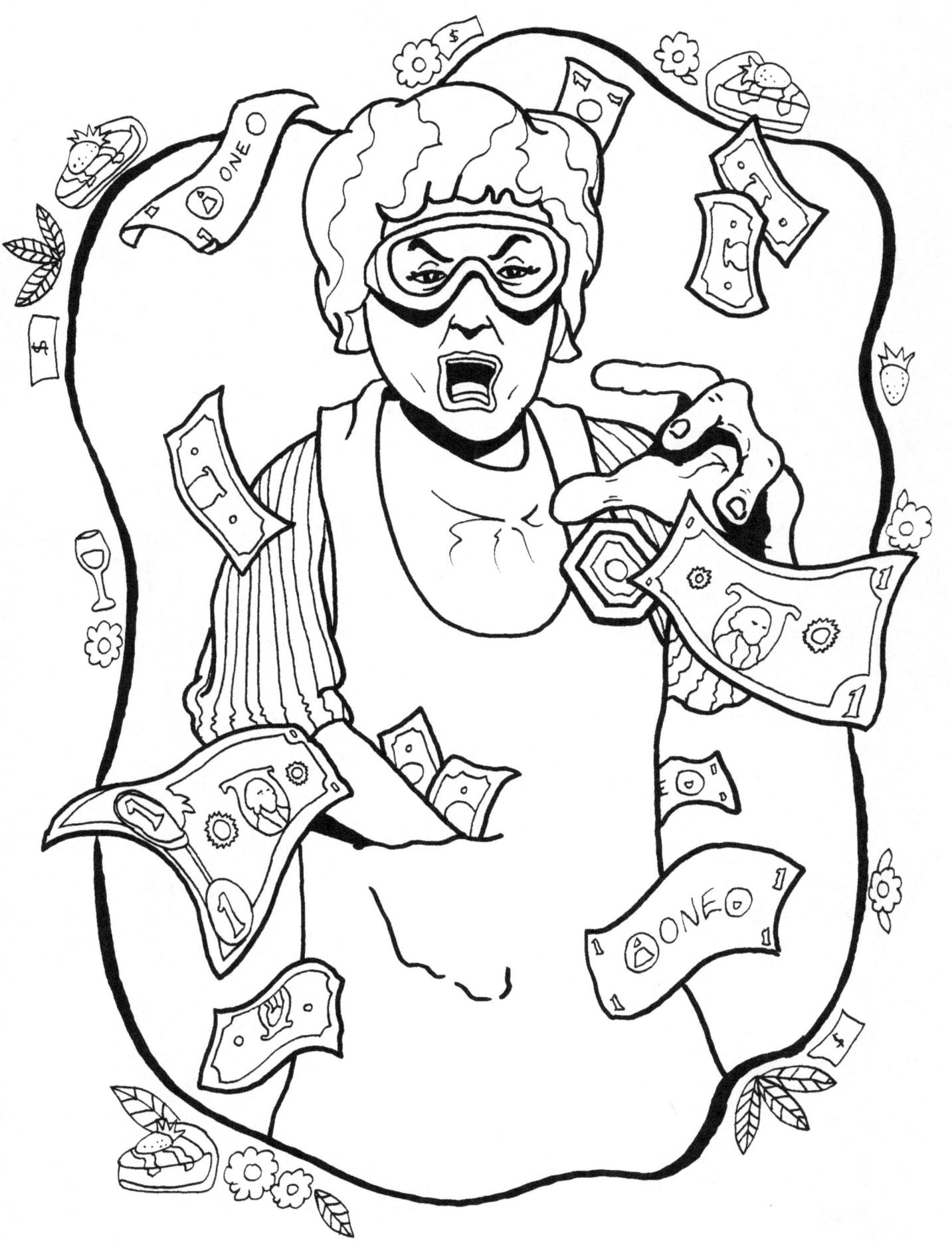

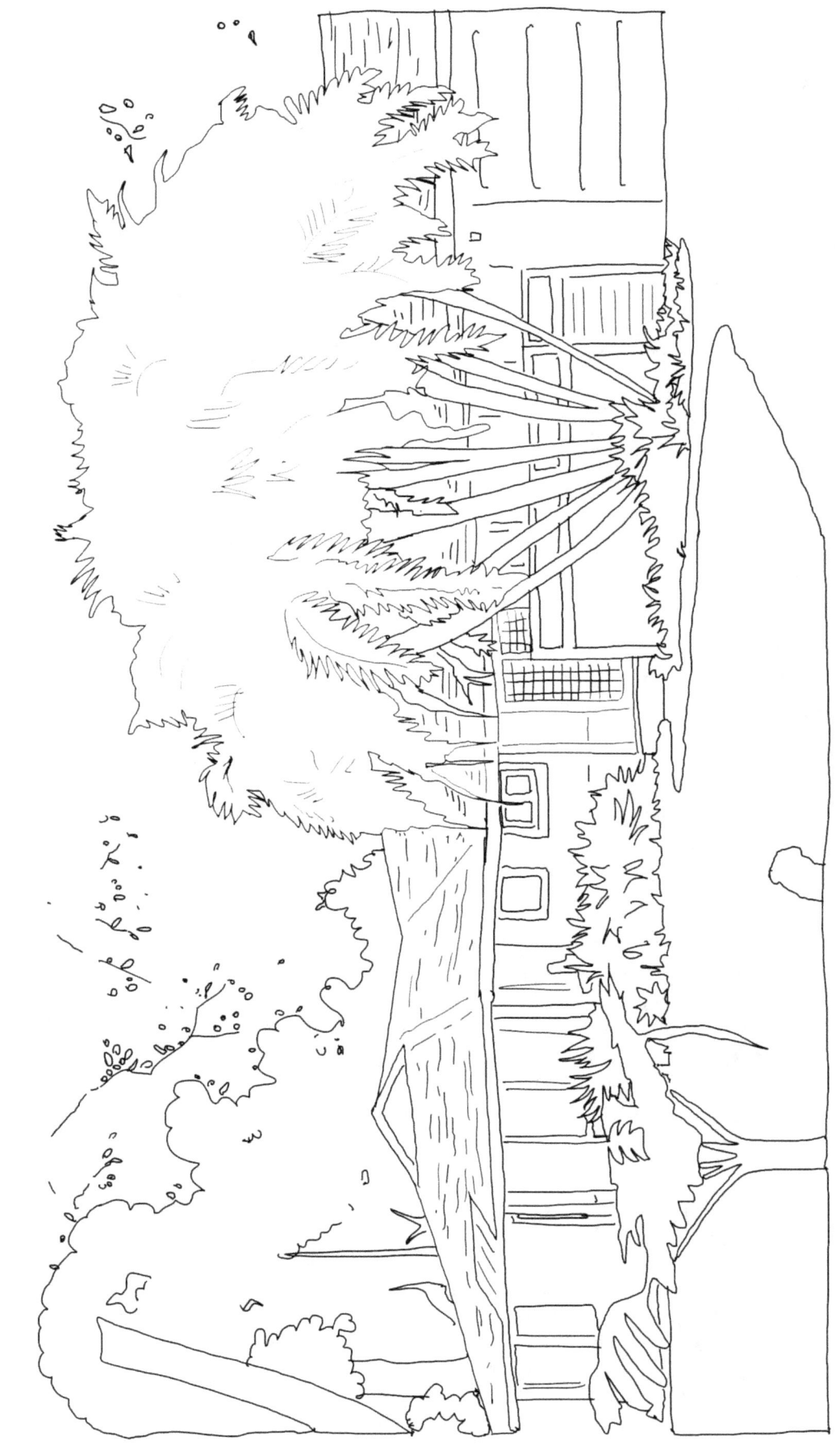

"One-Line" Drawings

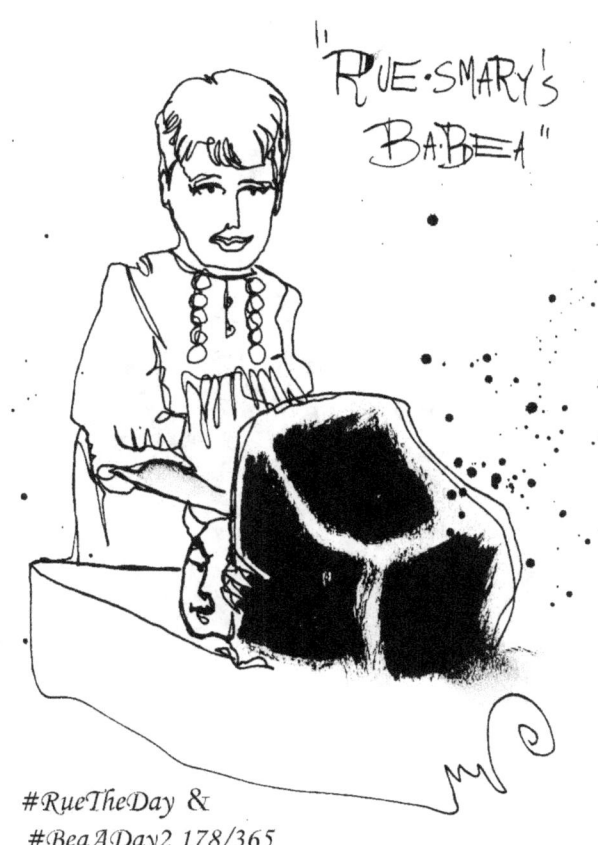

"RUE·SMARY'S BA·BEA"

#RueTheDay &
#BeaADay2 178/365

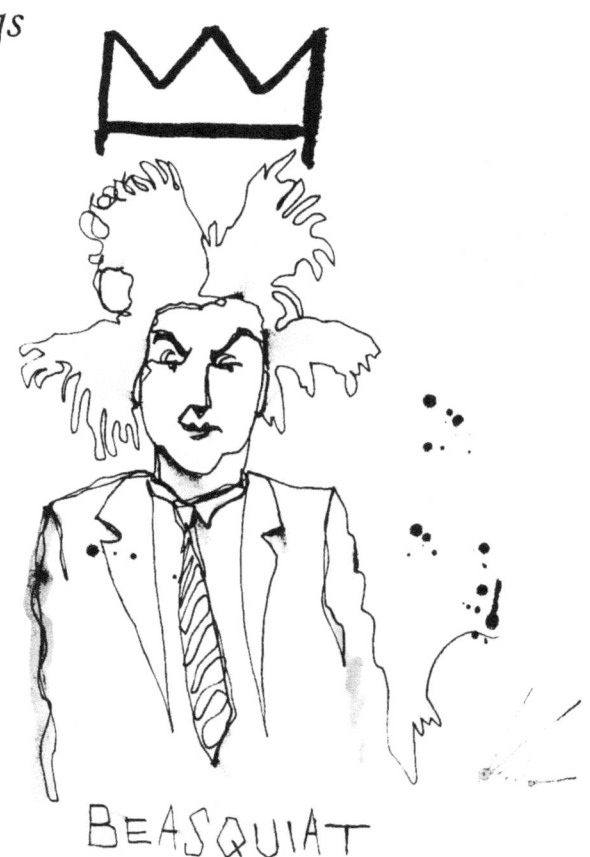

BEASQUIAT

#BeaADay2 84/365

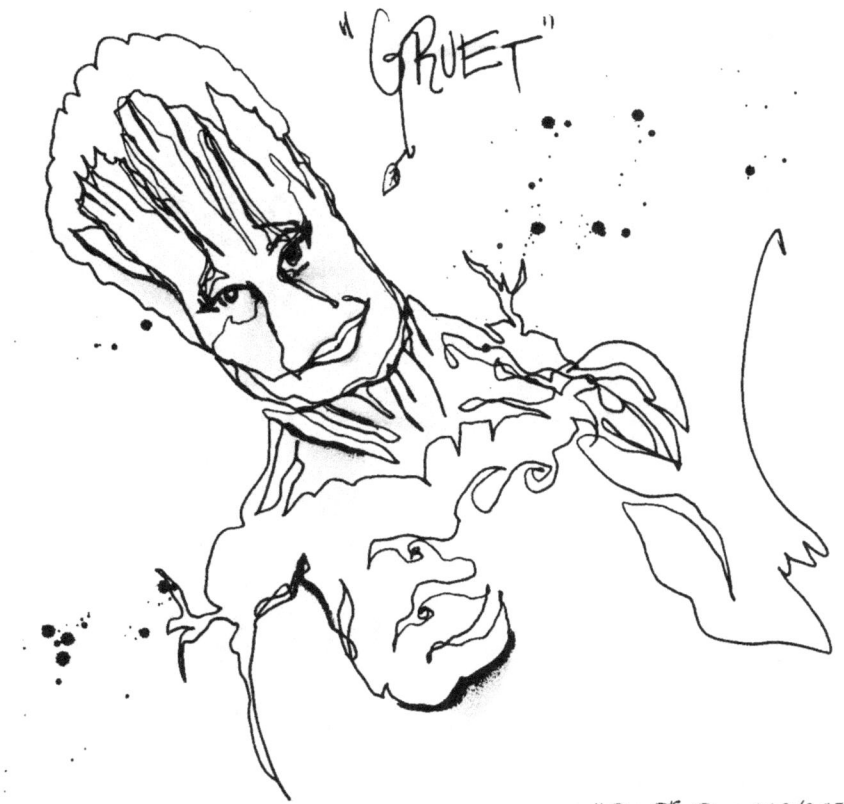

"GRUET"

#RueTheDay 118/365

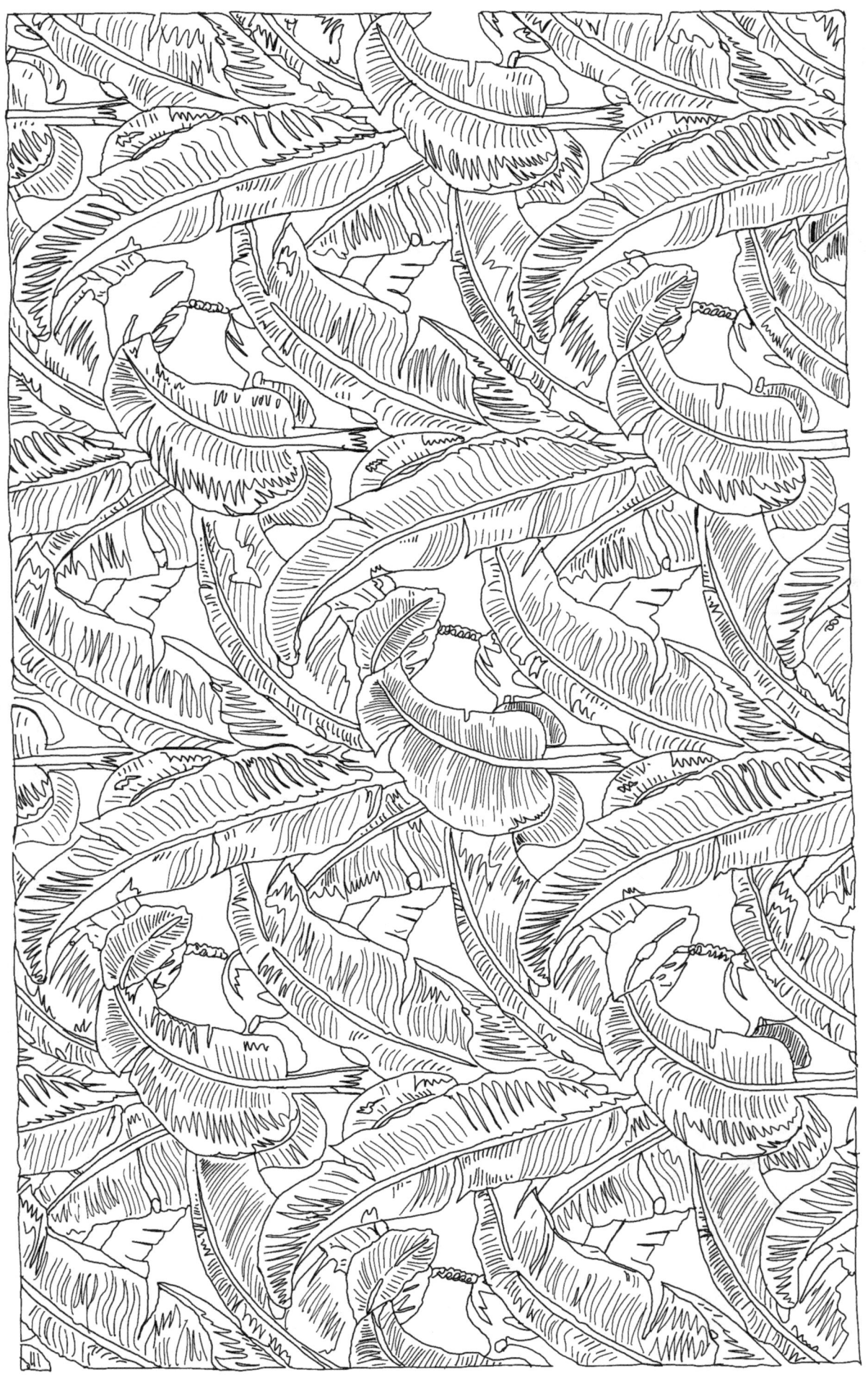

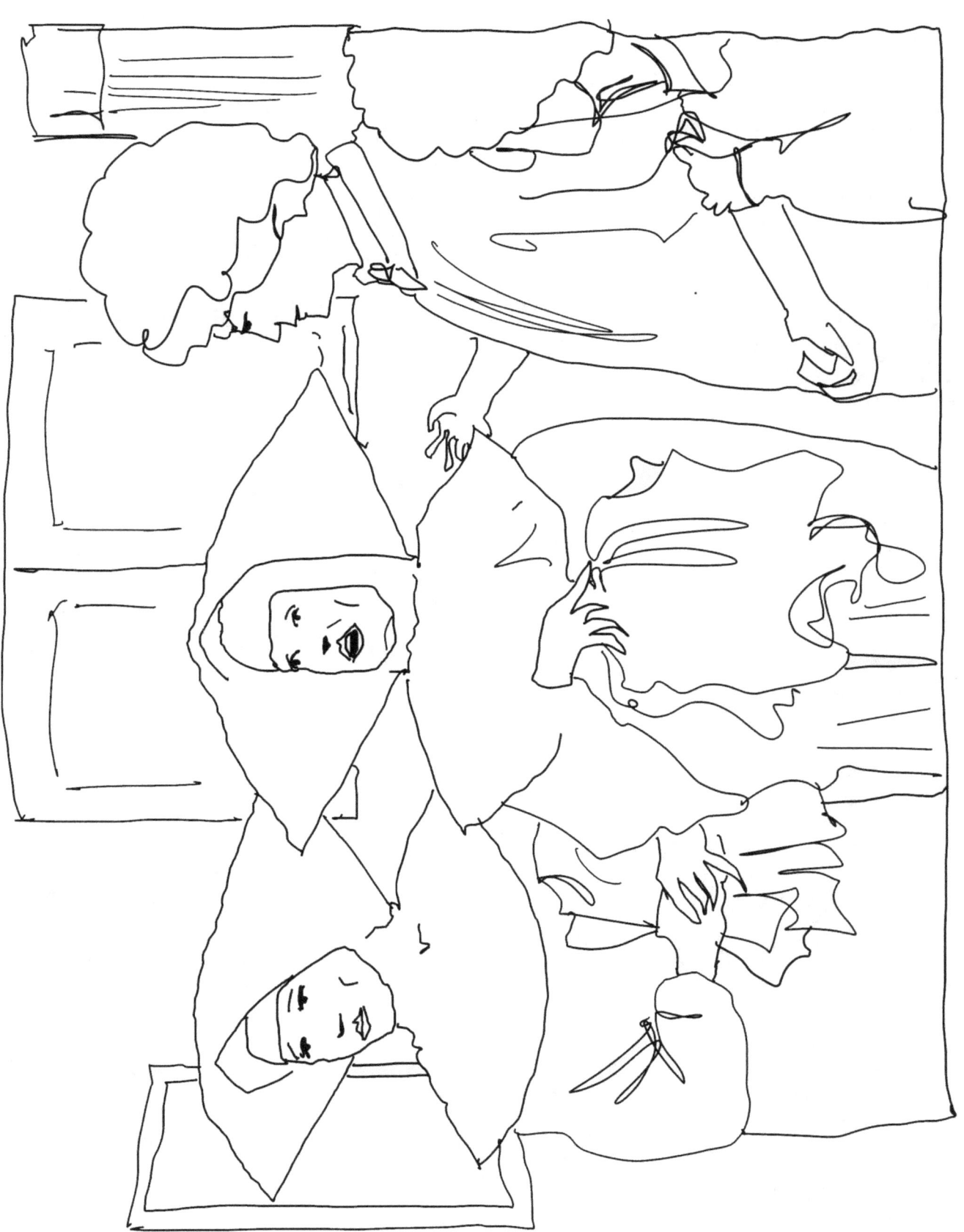

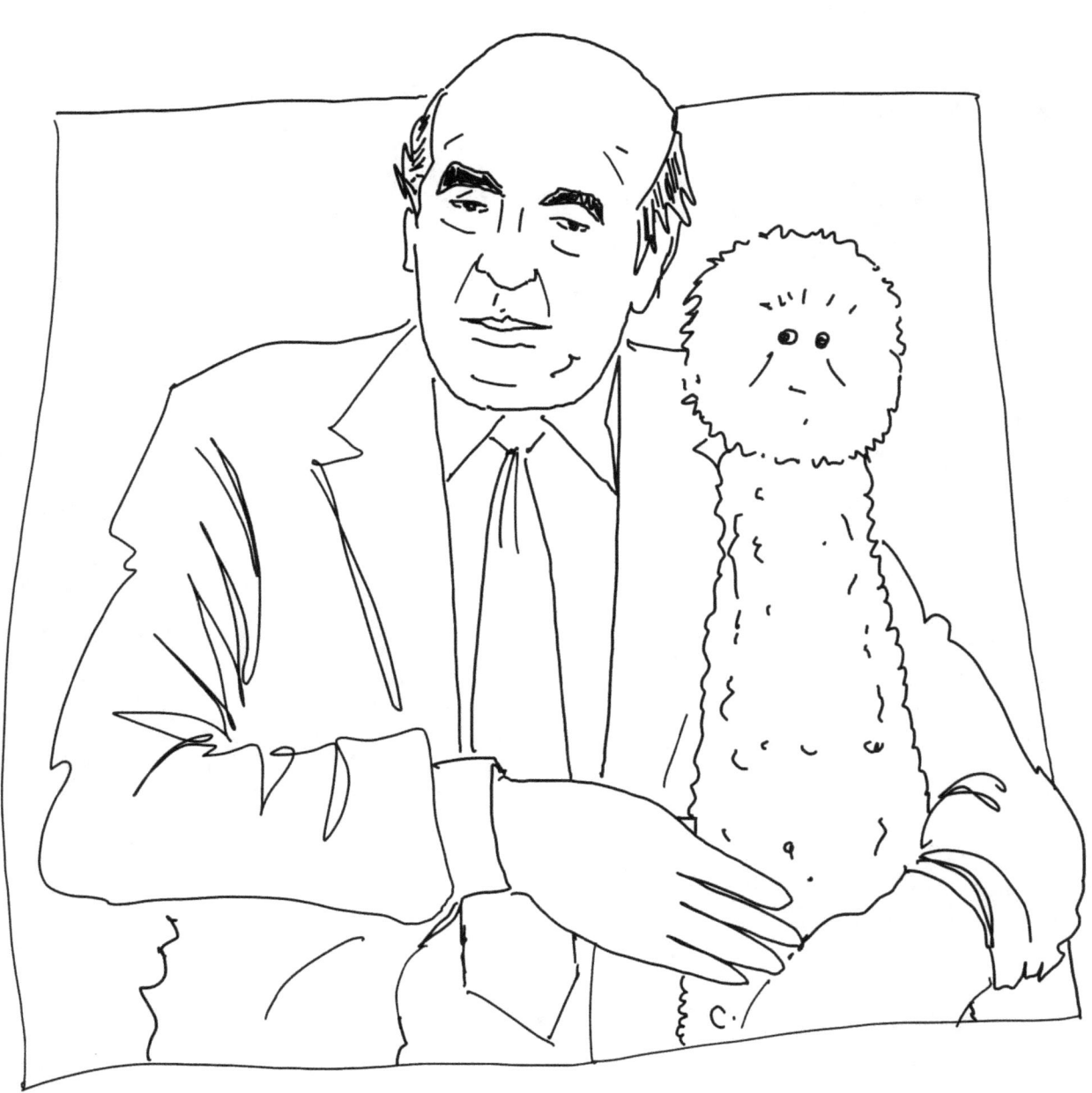

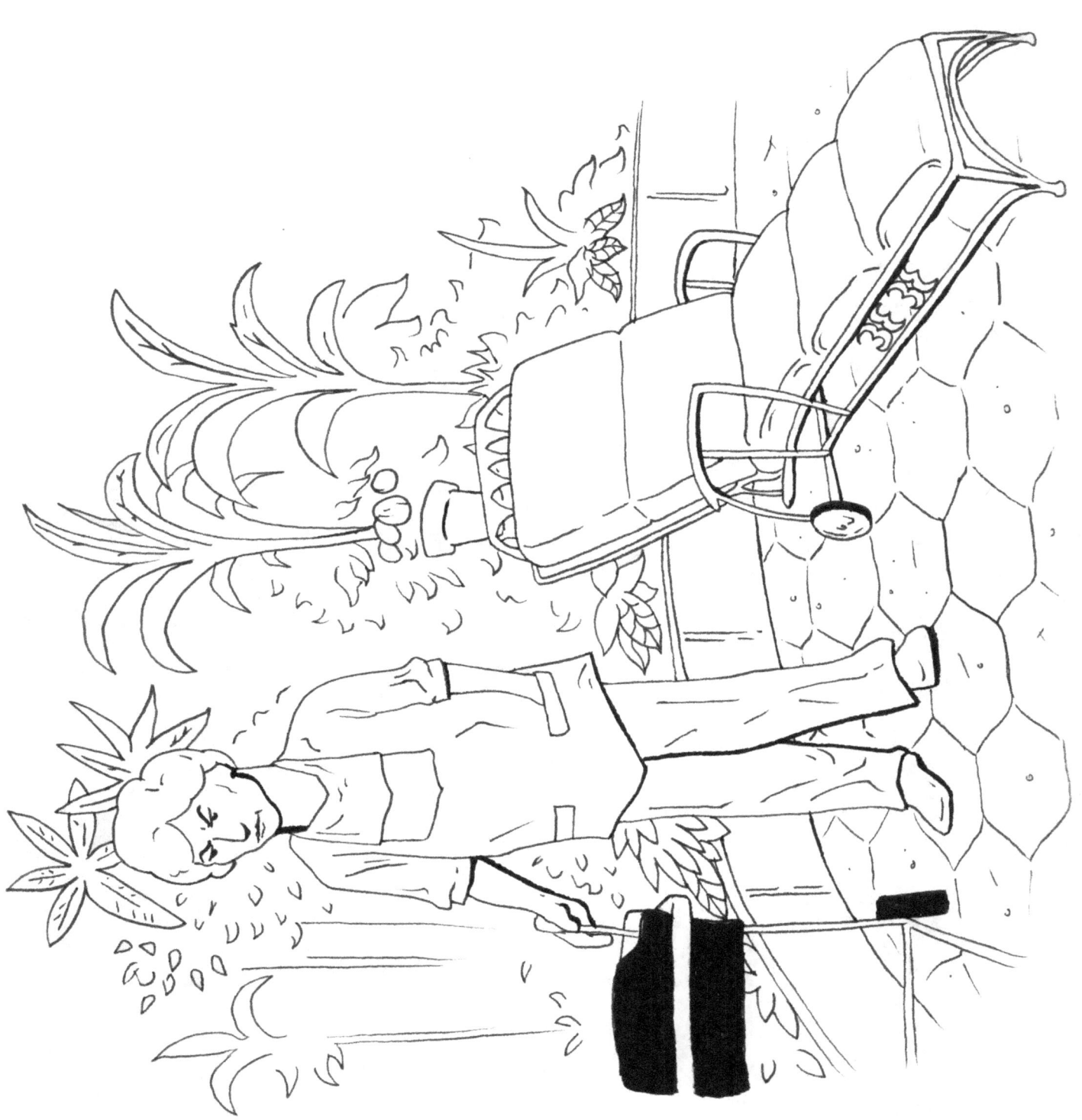

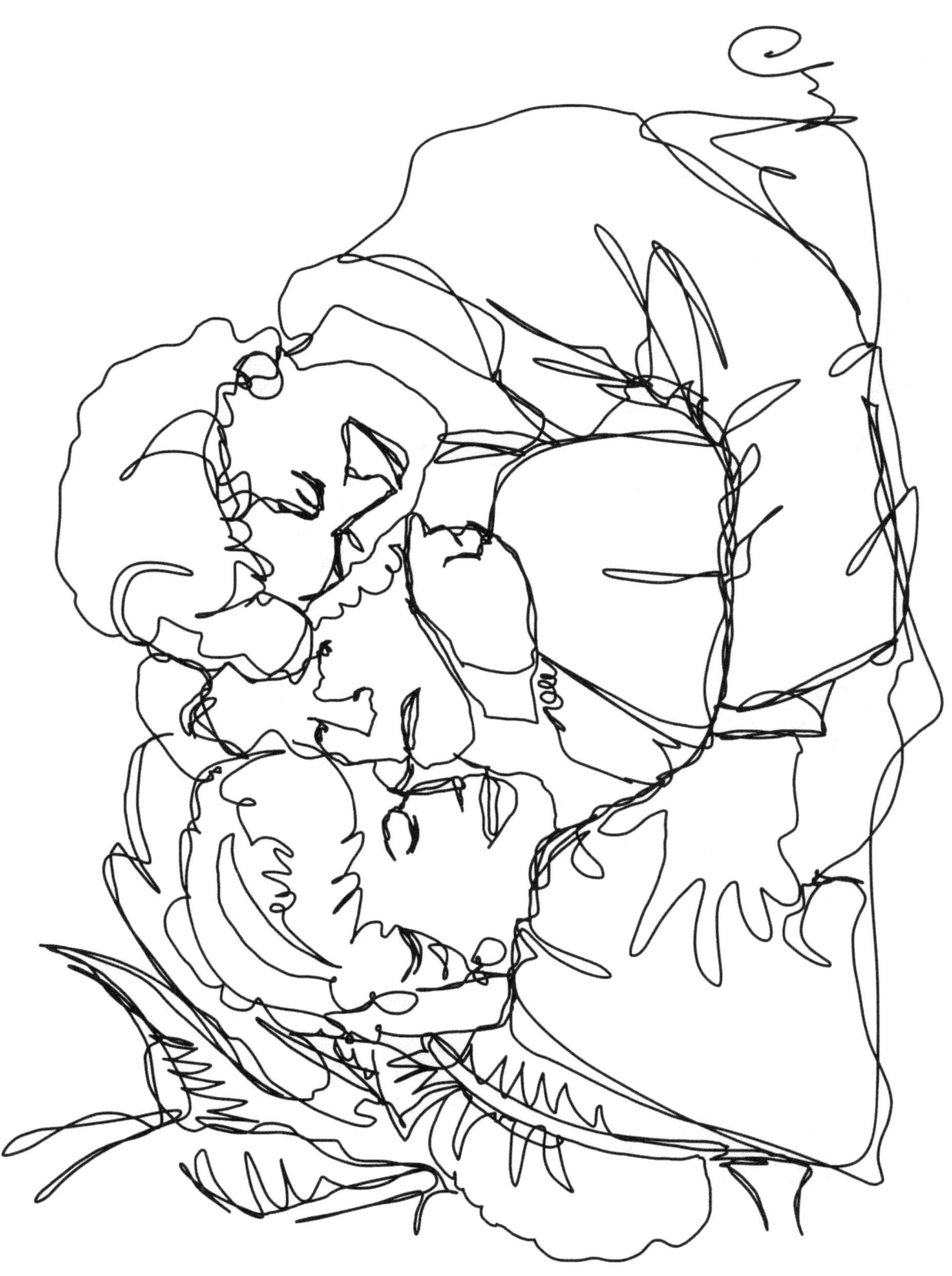

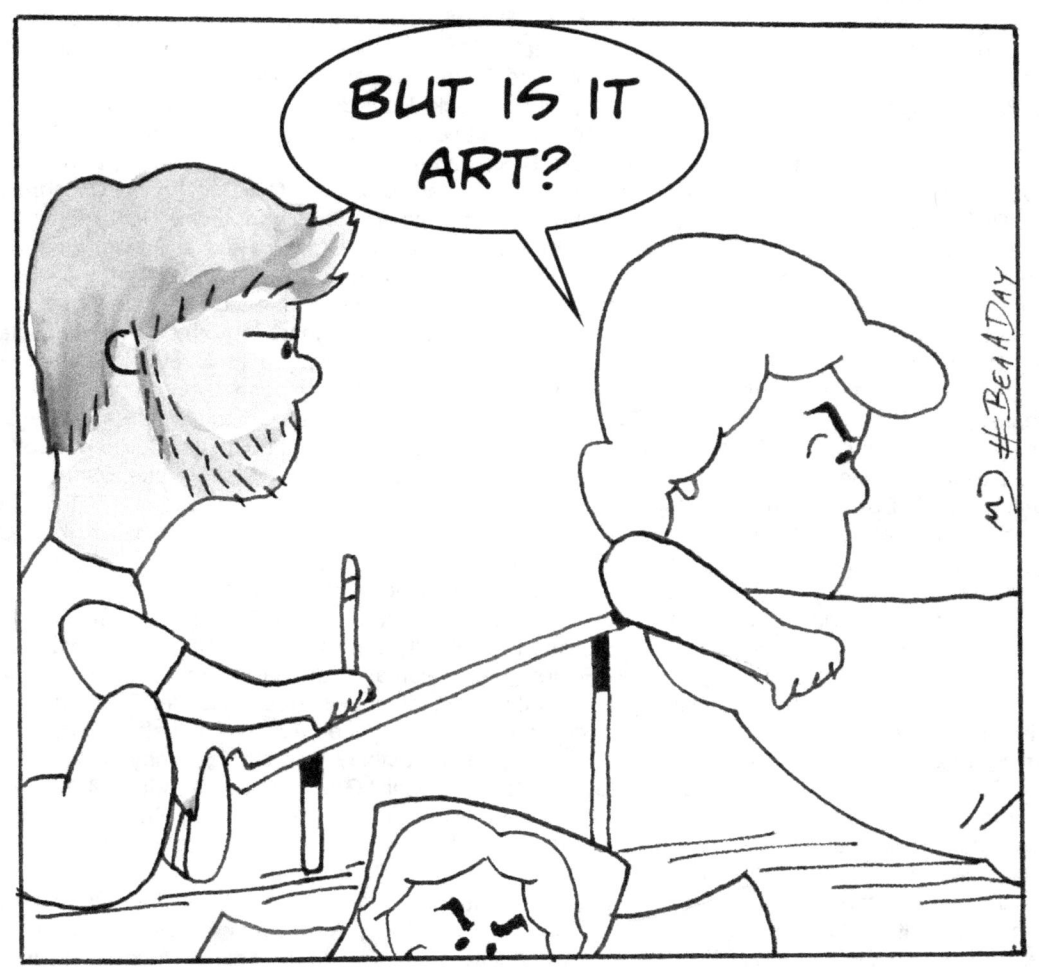

About the Author

Mike Denison lives near Boston, MA, with his wife, 2 sons and dog. So far he has only penned one *About the Author* piece.
This is it.

Find more info about Mike's art projects at:
www.themikedenison.com
shop.BeaADay.com
& @mikd33 on the social medias

THANK YOU FOR BEING A FRIEND: Matt Abruzzo, Jenny Abshire-Eberly, Ady, Aki & Roland, Annerys Alba, Alexius, Alishea, Ray Allen, Jackie Alvarez, Lawrence Alvarez, Brandy M. Amos, Christina Anderson, John Anderson, Susie Anderson, Lou Andrade, Annemarie, Apple & BooBoo, Eddie Arias, Cat Armato, Carl John Armbruster, Matt Armstrong, Tyler Auck, Audrey or Odd, Aunt Tomato, Tara B., Kimberly Swihart Balakrishnan, Allen Ball, Laura Balletto, Samuel D. Banford, Jennifer Barber, Yvonne Britton Barner, Carolyn Barrett, Barbara & Kelly, Beal Street Party Palace, Alexandra Beaverhausen, Aubrey Nicole Beck, Roni Beck, Jason Becker, Becky, Keigh-Cee Welsch Bell, Tony Bell, Michael Bellew, Michael Bennett, Tyler Starlord Benson, Ashley Berman, Brian David Berman, "Best Boss Ever" Gerry, Jen Bjerke, Eric Blackman, Liza Blackman (or whatever you want mike), Erin "Bea" Blanton, Kate Blaylock, Mike Blaylock, Saidah Blount, Jana Bodner, Tristan Z Bolden, Colleen "Freida Claxton" Bonner, Tiffany Bowie, Phil Bradford, William D. Bradshaw, Joshua Branch, Shawna Bridgforth, Lynne Bright, Bring Me Sugar Shop, Amy Jo Brixius, Rob Brodeur, David Brooks, Elizabeth Abigayle Brown, Gladys Brown, Spencer Brown, Matt Browning, Angel Bruno, Burbunny, David Burke-Moore, Isaac Burrough, Andrew C., Angie C., Erin C., Meaghan Callahan, Julie Cannon, Leah Cannon, CapnWook, Becky Capps, Rob Capriccioso, Jen Caprio, Chad & Charles Carfagno, Shanna Carlson, Sara Carpinone, Adam Casey, Kelly Castagnaro, Jeremy Cates, Marisela Caylor, Sarah Cazier, D. Chambers, Elisa M. Chambers, Molly Chambers, Grace Cheung, John Chevrier, Chonch, Anthony Cicero, Amanda Clack, Jennifer Cleland, Ashleigh Cocke (Sophia PeKILLo), Megan Lynn Condon, Neal Conner, Gary Contessa, Charles Cook, Shelley Cook, Tammy Costrini, Courtney & Chris, April Crabtree, Kaye Crawford, Jamie Cross, Norma Crowther, The Crushed Violet Fragrance Boutique, Sherial Cubit, Dan Cullinan, Scott Cunniff, Tarrah Curtis, Dustin Cushman, Erica D., Kate D, Paula D., DJ Mary Fresh, Dr. Steve, Jake Dann, D'Artagnan Nicole Dantes, Tyler J. Davis, Jenny DeBiasio, Maggie de la Cruz, George Delvalle, Debbie & Todd Denison, Laurel Denison, Adam DeRosa, Whitney DeVilbiss, Brian Devlin, Marilyn Monica Angela Maria Di Toro, Cassidy Dimon, Craig S Dorfman, Refinnej Dornooc, Doug & Eddie, Tracey Dougherty, Wendy Drinkwater, Cassandra Duck, Heather Duench-Dye, Robyn Bussey Dunn, Maria Duran, Becca E, echo, Miriam Edelstein, The Edwards Family, Mathew Edwards, Elizabeth & Erin, Meredith Elkin, Sean Elliott & Will Brattain, Jamie Zbornak Erdheim, Patrick Esteban, Katy Esquivel, Kathleen Evans, Christiane Evaskis-Garrett, Daniel "Pussycat" Ewald, Kaitlen Jay Exum & Jordan Young, Jordan F. & Dan N., Brayden Falgout, Julie Felder, Jake Feldman, Sabrina M. Feldman, Samantha Ferris, Travis Fessler, Joshua Finnell, Rory K. Fish, Sean M Fitzgerald, Ron Fitzherbert, Rachel Fitzpatrick, Jess & Debbie Flamholz, Ryanleo Flores, Heather Foley, Julene Fontaine, Tara Foster, Ashley Frechette, Mark Frechione, Lindsey Frimming, Elizabeth Frost, Lamar Zbornak Fuller, Deepee G, Justin G. & Keith P., Kenny G, Mark G., Stephanie G, Megan Gallegos, Danielle Gallo, Mike Ganino, Sara "Fourth Chair" Gauchat, Mondi, Ariana & Nadia Ghasedi, Doug Giffin, Katie Gea Gillum, Rob Giordano, Toni Gisone, Alison Glancz, Jennifer and Rhonda Glover, Valerie Pajak Glyptis, Adam Reilly Gobble, Marc S. Goldberg, Golden Girls 4Ever ~Dennis W., Brenda Goll, Melanie Gonick, Ben Goretsky, Jessica Gotsch, Grace, Ed Grady, Barbara Graham, Tiffany Grayson, Andi Greco, Adriane Grey, Anjo Griffith, Ann Gustafson, Lindsay Gutekunst, Galo R. Gutierrez, Tanya Gutierrez, Melanie Linn Gutowski, Amber L. Guyton, Hailey, K J Hagans, Zanna Haines, Danny Haloossim, Karen Hamberg, Evin Hamilton, Happy birthday Lauren Fields and Sarah Lewis!, Draper Harlow, Marissa Harrison, Mark Hartzell, Have a Romy & Michelle Day, David Havelick, ☆ Jill & Brian Healey ☆, Juha Heikkila, Abby Heilbron, Helene, Jennifer Hendzlik, Maya and Natalie Herman, Hi Mom, Darcy and Daphne Hicks, Andrew Hiener, Brandi Leigh Hill, Kim Hill, Hillymack, Faith Hoenstine, Tishauna Hoffman & Nicole Beach, Caroline Li Holland, Suzann Holland, the holmes boy, Laura Houser, Leslie E. Howerton, Ann Hudspeth, Gwyneth Hughes, Laurel Hunter, Amandita Hutch, Adrienne Hwee, Jason Hyatt, Iannacone & McKnight Families, P.J. Iannelli, Sherri Ievers, Charlotte Innerd, Nicole Irene, Nicole D. Jackson, Nathan James, Jamie the Naive One, jasonburglar, Alex Jenne, Jess, Jesús, Jillian, Joey, Joey & Cait, Delray Johnson, Crista Marie Jones, Danielle Joy, Just Cara, Justin, Cindy K., Rich K!, K-Slice, Wanda Kaiser, Ciara "Don't Touch My Foot" Karski, Brianne & Jessie Karten, Kate, Bailey Kaupang, Tory Kay, Erin Keaveney, Jenn Keaveney, Sarah Keesler, Tracy Kellett, Kelly & Shauntelle #GG4Life, John Kelly, Tina Kemp, Hayden O. Kepley III, Kyle R. Keppel, Kelly Kessler, Melania & Roya Khouie-Vargas (Best Buds), Kim, John King, Catie, Corey & Susan Kinger, Jonny "Chi" Kirmani, Jennie Knies, Greg Koch, Komé, Trena Kostantinovich, Molli Kreuser, Kristen, Kristen and Angela 4/22/17, Kristen & Tutu, Joseph La Corte, Maeve S. Lant, Leah, Steve Leichman, Brandon Lemoine, Emily Lent, Kimberly Lepovsky, Will Leubsdorf, Marie Liebetrau, Leigh Lilla, Tricia Linley, Deena Loeffler, Katie Lorenzo, LMR, Jaime Luermann, Lyle Lulich, Sara Lunt, Andrea Lynn, David Lyons, Mandy M, Paul Magowan, Jalila Maldonado, Ryann Malone, Mariospeedwagon: Noe & Heather, Christina Mancusi, Amy Margaret, Mariette, Stacia Marlett, B E Marshall, Elizabeth Martin, Stephen J. Martin-Bennet, Enrique Mas, Matt and Viviana, Starla Dawn McCarty, Dr. Boots McCann, K80 McClellan, Sarah McCue, The McDowells, Wade McGarity, Brian McKee, Patrick Austin McLynch, Sean McMahill, Tony Medina, MeeMaw, Bobby Mendenhall, Mike & Justin - 91314, Allison Miller, Aaron Millman, Al Minghella, Jessica Mingolelli, Monera, Rosealba Monticello, Justin Moore, Gillian Morshedi, MsRachelSF, Anthony Murisco, C I Murphy, Rachelle Murphy, Nicole Mustaccio, Ashley Myers Number One Golden Girls Fan, Myschyf, Vickey Napier, Richard Naples, Carolyn Nelson, EG Nelson, Morgan R. Nelson, Nik Nemec, Edward Newman, Nicholas, J. Nobley, Wm. Noffsinger, Garrett Norris, Shaun F. Noworyta, Missy Nowak, Kelsey Oates, Diane L. Odeh,

Russell Britt Oden Jr, Robyn Okrant, Old Ladies ROCK!, Anne Olson, Lucia Ortner, Chris Overholt, Marisa Overton, Padgett and Kara, Natasha Padilla, Treightin Palimenio, Joe Paquette, Jamie L. Parker, Stephanie Parker, S. N. Parks, Anita Patel, Patrick, Danery Pawson, Scott Pearson, Kristen Peck, Em Perry, Haley Elizabeth Perry, Randy & Tony Phillips-Womble, Philip Pierce, Suzy Pietras-Smith, Jessi Pitrelli, Amanda Platt, John Plunkett, Kate Porter, Lisa Porter, Ben Posner, Tracy Prather, Keith Preble, Audrey E Pritchard, Louis J Prizzi, Rad Probst, Dianne Puhr, Laura Quinzi, Meredith R., Amanda Rachels, Jessica Marie Radke, Tiffany & Jessie Rauch-Dickson, Simon Rawls, Ray, Reblecha, Lauren M. Reese, Ken Reid, Marie Reilly, Maxwell Roahrig, Christen Rhody, Rhonda, Gail Richardson, Emily "Dorothy" Rick, Kristina Rigney, Rishan "Fish", Rene Rivers, Robbie and Tauni, Fleming Roberts, Lacy Roberts, Susan Roberts, Carl L. Rodig, Alberto Rodriguez-Marcano, Dina Rogers, Ron, Cherelynore Roosevelt, Ada Rose, Leanna Rose, Nicole Rosen, Sarah Shafer Rosenbaum, Karen Rosenberg, Leslie Rosenberg, Nikki Rosenberg, Sarah Rubens, Rob Ruetsch, Keon Ruiter, Christine M. Ruiz, Pasquale E. Rummo, Taylor Russo, Eric Safdieh-Nelson, George Salloum, Paola Sampang, Taylor Sampson, Guido Alexander Sanchez, Tim Sandusky, Robert & Sven Saunders-Janssen, Reeny Savage, Jen Schenk, Lisa Schaffner, Nicole Schlenk, Kate Schmidt, Sara Schultz, Amanda Schuster, John "skoles" Scullin, Kari Scullin, Marty Severino, Jeffrey Sgro & Robert Beaubien, Beth Shaw, Jill Shelton, Kristin Sheppard, Rebecca Shirley, Oliver Shreeve, Ethan Siegel, Melanie S. Simmons, LeeAnne Sipe, Lauren Sir, Kayla Slater, Aimee M. Smith, Ben Smith, David Sommer, SoKeR1bostonATL, Kate Sorensen, Josh Soto, Garrett Sparks, Jennifer Spiegelman, Lauren Spigno, Dan Spinner, Brian Spoonemore, Brandon Stalnaker, Catherine Crump Stead, Tommy Stemper, Susan Stephens, Jeri Sterling, Matthew Stevens, Amy Stevens-Pickell, Stivness, Melissa Stocker, Gretchen Stokka, Kristi "Rose" Stroh, Chris Strok, Erin Sullivan, Jen Sun, Super Nanny, Superior Angie, Kristen Swanson, Maria T., Mike Tague & Andrew Mercier, Julie El Taher, Christopher A. Taylor, #TeamNoBabies, Ben Templar, Lauren Elizabeth Tennant, Lara Tesh, Thadtastic, Thom @ http://1980s.me, Liz Thomas, Tiffany & Dru, Tue Tran, T. E. Trimble, Greg Trocola-Barone, Nathan Tucker, Sarah Tunks, Elena Tzerefos-Parks, Ajshe Va-Dada Pllana, Sailesh Vaghela, Wade Valdez, Krystle Valentin, Chrisse Rubenstein Van, Christopher Vasques, Julie Vaughn, Amanda Villa, Nancy Marie Villegas, Murray Von Kittypants, Dr. Jenny Wagner, Brent Walden, Larissa Walker, Ralph Walker II, Lynn Wallace, Christi Wampler, Jen Wangler, Michael M Ward, Russell W. Warnick, Greg Watson, Joseph and Lilian Watson, Justin Webb, Molly Wee, Sarah Weinberger-Litman, George G. Weiss & Don Shaw, Amanda 'Bea' Williams, Lynn Trotta Williams, Patricia Williams, Tarah Williams & Lindsey Theodorakis, Matt Willson, Alison Wisneski, Andrew Woodworth, Jessica Yankowski, Evelyn EJ Yates, Kristen Yorty, Young Beezy, Joe Young, Margaret Yurkov, Barbara Z, Carl Zbornak, Stan Zbornak, John T. Zeiler, Mandy Zeller, Zulu: Queen of the Dwarf People

EXTRA SPECIAL THANKS TO: Jim Colucci, Ryan Coy, Frank DeCaro, Jack Denison, Jack E. Denison, Jon Denison, Laura Denison, Mary Jane Denison, Sam Denison, Kerri Doherty, David Filipov, Carrie Fisher, Bobby Gaylor, Matthew Gilbert, Lucretia Gisone, Eliot Glazer, Charles Halford, Chris Hardwick, Theresa Hwang, Sophea Khem, Brian Kokernak, Maureen Mansfield, Noah Michelson, Christina Palumbo, Dave Rubin, H. Alan Scott, Rich Shertenlieb, Jay Thomas, Fred Toucher, Ricky Velez, Larry Wilmore, Curtis Wong

AND OF COURSE: Bea Arthur, Estelle Getty, Rue McClanahan & Betty White

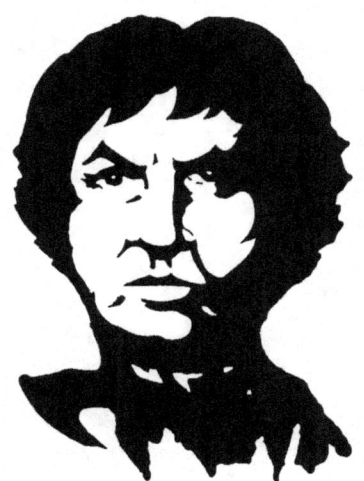